THE BLOCKBUSTER BIBLE

THE TEACHER'S CUT

BEHIND THE
SCENES OF THE
BIBLE STORY

I will utter hidden things, things from of old –
things we have heard and known,
things our ancestors have told us.
We will not hide them from their descendants;
we will tell the next generation
the praiseworthy deeds of the Lord,
his power, and the wonders he has done.

Psalm 78:2–4 [NIV]

Tell me, I'll forget.
Show me, I'll remember.
Involve me, I'll understand.

A Chinese proverb

CONTENTS

Prologue 5

The Bible Story: Three Themes 8

The Bible Story: Scene by Scene 11

Lights, Camera, Action! 16

Guide to Production Notes 18

Guide to Action Plans 19

Unit Guides 20

Photocopiable Activity Sheets 72

Published by
Lion Hudson Limited
Wilkinson House, Jordan Hill Business Park
Banbury Road, Oxford OX2 8DR, England
www.lionhudson.com

ISBN 978 0 7459 7823 9

First edition 2020

Acknowledgements
Original design and illustration by Collaborate for *The Blockbuster Bible*
With thanks to The Bible Project for their permission to reference their videos in this book.

A catalogue record for this book is available from the British Library

Printed and bound in China, October 2019, LH54

PITCH

The Blockbuster Bible is a Bible, study Bible, and Bible overview hybrid. It can be used to teach the Bible story to anyone aged 7+, while *The Teacher's Cut* supports teachers to use it in their context. The course is not age-specific, but it has been written with 7–11s in mind. The blockbuster movie theme connects the whole story. Good movies have similar story arcs: harmony, fall, redemption, and new beginning. The visual mediums present the texts in a fun way and remind the reader of the connectedness of the whole story.

The Teacher's Cut supplies the teacher with tools for the job. It gives lesson ideas, not lesson plans. A menu, not a recipe! Production Notes give unit aims, content, and background information. Action Plans give activities that work with the content, with supporting sheets at the back. The material enables teachers to be creative as they use it – so children can enjoy reading the Bible.

PROGRAMME

Teachers and children can follow the Bible story in one of two ways. They can follow the 24 scene cards running through *The Blockbuster Bible*, or they can follow the three themes. Each one gives children simple ways of engaging with the story. The scene cards summarize each section of the story using everyday images. The three themes have logo stickers that pop up throughout the book; teachers and children can follow these to plot the storylines. See pages 8–15 for full retellings through each lens.

The Blockbuster Bible is written for multiple contexts: homes, schools, and churches. The pages are laid out in simple two-page spreads: the left and right pages aim to complement each other and work as pairs. The two questions on each page help to unpack what is going on. Read how 3D Freddie and Popcorn Sally answer common questions, and read the flashbacks and flash-forwards to make the connections between stories.

The Blockbuster Bible and *The Teacher's Cut* applies a cross-curricular approach. These books aim to develop key skills (questioning, linking, thematizing, discussing, and creating). Children can read the Bible on their own, and it supports English, Literacy, History, Geography, ICT, and Music. Longer chapters in *The Blockbuster Bible* allow teachers to be selective and also set extension work. The framework allows higher achievers to cover more material, while others still understand the main concept.

The Blockbuster Bible has limitations. The three themes and 24 scene cards are just one interpretation. The absence of personal application questions may disappoint leaders in churches who want to apply the texts to growing personal faith and prayer. The selection of stories is thorough but not complete (for example, Job is missing). And some may find the modern/movie mediums distracting. But the book has a simple aim: to engage a modern audience with the Bible's ancient message.

PLANNING

Option 1: two-term course

Work through the 24 scene cards in order. Cover the Old Testament in the autumn term and the New Testament in the spring term. This is quick, and the Old Testament naturally leads up to Christmas, and the New Testament to Easter. Suggestion: teachers should count their lessons for a term and allocate a scene for each lesson or two lessons. Plan in project time (e.g. on Jesus' miracles).

Option 2: two-year course

Cover a more thorough selection of texts across four terms.

Year 1: Old Testament Acts 1–4
New Testament Act 6: Scenes 1–4

Year 2: Old Testament Act 5
New Testament Act 6: Scenes 5–8

Other groupings may work. Focus more on the three themes of the Bible story: *Living with God, God's Promises*, and *God's Rescue*. Find links between the Old and New Testament selections (e.g. link the prophets' message in Act 5 with the disciples' message in Act 7). Be careful not to make links too contrived and confusing.

Option 3: theme by theme

Trace the three themes. This may work better with more able, familiar, or independent learners. Look for the sticker logos for *Living with God, God's Promises*, and *God's Rescue*, and produce a project or presentation covering each one. Individuals, pairs, or groups may study a theme each, or all three themes. Alternatively, the teacher may teach a series of lessons on each theme to provide three overviews of the Bible story. For example:

Living with God: 1) the Garden of Eden and banishment; 2) tabernacle and Temple; 3) Jesus, friend of sinners; 4) the Spirit at Pentecost; 5) the new creation in Revelation 21 and 22.

God's Promises: 1) snake crusher and Abrahamic and Davidic Covenants; 2) messianic prophecies; 3) the New Covenant; 4) the Christians' inheritance; 5) the new creation in Revelation 7.

God's Rescue: 1) sin in the Garden of Eden; 2) the Exodus; 3) the cross and resurrection; 4) the Great Commission and spread of the gospel; 5) Paul explains how Jesus saves.

Option 4: single-Act/Scene term

Teachers may be pressed for time, or want to cover an Act or Scene for a term in more depth. Longer Acts lend themselves well to this (e.g. Act 5: Prophets and Kings, or Act 6: The Promised King).

PAGES

The Teacher's Cut aims to provide teachers with the tools for the job. For each unit there are Production Notes (background guides for the teacher) and Action Plans (an activity menu). See pages 19–20 for guides on these. There are also photocopiable sheets from page 72. Many of these are Flexi-Tasks: they can be used on many different topics – they do not refer to any individual story (storyboarding/movie poster/movie certificate, for example).

PROGRESS

What does progress look like in RE? Children will learn facts and stories through reading *The Blockbuster Bible*, but progress should not only involve knowing more. Children must also improve their skills. Children love to see themselves get better at things through challenging activities and repeatable (and varied) activities.

The Teacher's Cut offers plenty of writing, speaking, and creative tasks to help children grow their skills, if carefully repeated and made more challenging. For example, use the Scene Card Starter for a variety of writing or speaking options or use a Flexi-Task a few times to see progression. Work in line with your marking policy, or decide on marking criteria (for example, an ABC scheme with five marks available for: Accuracy, Brevity, Creativity). Alternatively, a small range of acting exercises appear throughout the book; repeat, vary, and review the activities (and film them) to show progress. You could consider your own criteria, which show growth of intelligence through strategies, practice, hard work, and input from others.

This book consciously does not offer anything in terms of progress or achievement tracking; it offers teacher's guides, activities, and sheets to support teaching, rather than a full curriculum with assessment objectives and outcomes, etc. Feel free to use this resource in whichever way it supports your context.

PRODUCTION

When I began *The Blockbuster Bible*, I wrote it primarily as a school textbook. I began teaching RE in 2008 and found a great shortage of Bible-teaching resource books written for schools. I really wanted to get children reading Bibles and understanding the whole story. Since then it has become a children's Bible, but you may spot some hallmarks of a school textbook.

A Bible overview seemed the best place to start. It's ironic how unfamiliar people are with the bestselling book of all time, even if they are familiar with some of its episodes (like Daniel and the lions, or David and Goliath). I love the movie world, and the movie theme seemed a great way to tell the story. Meet the stars of the greatest story ever told! It's a blockbuster! Now let's take our seats and get rolling. Curtains!

LIVING WITH GOD

Living with God involves living under his authority. God makes Adam and Eve to live with him in the Garden of Eden, a place of "delight". They're delighted to rule over God's creation as vice-rulers. God promises that they will die if they eat from the tree of knowledge of good and evil, but they listen to the snake's lies and reject God's authority. This is sin. Sin leads to banishment, as God sends them east and away from the Garden. Soon sin leads to murder, death, violence, and rebellion, and God banishes Adam and Eve's children further away from him.

Enter Abraham. The people are lost without God, but God approaches Abraham and promises to show him to his own land. This is where God's people – Israel – will live with him; there is a future for them. But Jacob's family move to Egypt to avoid famine and are soon stuck in slavery. God meets Moses at the Burning Bush and says, "I will be with you" (Exodus 3:12). Moses will lead his people to be with God and worship him at Mount Sinai.

The people of Israel enjoy living with God through the tabernacle. The tabernacle is the portable tent where God lives – "the tent of meeting". When the cloud of his presence lifts above the tent, the people move camp. The tabernacle has two rooms: the Holy Place; and the Most Holy Place where God lives. The ark of the covenant symbolizes God's authority and earthly presence once more. Eventually, Solomon builds a Temple to replace the tabernacle. It's a glorious high point of the Bible story.

But Israel suffers banishment once more. In 586 BC, Babylon destroys Jerusalem and the Temple. The people are exiled almost 900 miles away, where they lament feeling separated from God. Ezekiel mourns until God promises new things: "I will put my Spirit in you and you will live, and I will settle you in your own land" (Ezekiel 37:14). After 70 years away, the people have returned to Jerusalem and await a Messiah.

Cut to Nazareth, centuries later. An angel tells a virgin she will have a child called Immanuel (meaning "God is with us"). Jesus is born and John says God dwells (or "tabernacles") among his people once more (John 1:14). He is the *incarnation* of God – God in the flesh. Jesus lives among those who will accept their need for him – sinners – while the religious leaders reject him. Jesus soon promises to send the Spirit to "be with you forever" (John 14:16).

At Pentecost, the Spirit comes to live within the disciples. God now makes his dwelling place (tabernacle) within all believers (Ephesians 2:22). God lives inside them to guarantee that they will live with God in the new creation (2 Corinthians 5:5). In the new creation, John sees that God lives with humankind and Jesus rules them from the throne. They live with God under his authority in perfect friendship once more. Everlasting delight!

GOD'S PROMISES

The Bible is full of promises and fulfilments. God promises Adam and Eve they will die if they eat from the tree… Aged 930, Adam dies, and the Bible follows this with a list of his descendants all dying. The curse of death affects all people, but God promises to deal with it. Still in Eden, he promises Eve a "snake crusher" from among her descendants, who will defeat the curse of sin and death and die in the process. This Chosen One, or Messiah, will deal with humankind's biggest problem.

God's covenants bring hope for a sinful and fallen world. Covenants are lasting promises or agreements. By Noah's time, the people's thoughts are only evil all the time and God regrets making them. He sends a flood to recreate the world. Afterward he makes the Noahic Covenant never to repeat it, marking his promise with a rainbow. He is promising to redeem his world rather than wipe it out again.

Enter Abraham! God promises him three things: land, nation, and blessing. God will show him where his people will live, and promises him countless descendants, like the stars in the sky and the sand on the seashore. God will bless Abraham's great nation and they will bless the earth. God marks his promise with circumcision – Abraham's nation must remember the promises.

When the nation of Israel meets God at Mount Sinai, he makes new promises to them. This covenant depends on them. He tells them that "if you obey me fully and keep my covenant, then you will be my treasured possession" (Exodus 19:5). The Mosaic Covenant, which Moses received on Sinai, promises Israel much but demands much. God promises many blessings for obedience and curses for disobedience.

Israel follows their godly King David, a man after God's heart. He plans to build a house for God, but God promises David a "house", a ruling dynasty that lasts forever (2 Samuel 7:8–17). The Davidic Covenant promises that a king will rule God's people for eternity. The people now wait for this Chosen One. The prophets make Messianic prophecies: he will be born from a virgin in Bethlehem and he will ride a colt into Jerusalem and die for people's sins (Isaiah 53:5).

Jesus fulfils four key prophecies on the cross. As the snake crusher, he ends the curse of death by carrying the blame for people's sin. Secondly, he fulfils the Abrahamic Covenant by blessing people with forgiveness. Thirdly, he fulfils the Mosaic Covenant by perfectly obeying the Law and bringing blessing. And lastly, he fulfils the Davidic Covenant by rescuing his people from sin and death, and bringing them before his throne in the new creation. He is a suffering king who defeats sin on his throne, the cross, wearing a crown of thorns.

The new creation sees Jesus enthroned in God's new Eden. He rules and cares for his people from the throne, and his people from many nations gather around him. They are blessed with pure white robes. God fulfils all his promises in Jesus, who is a shepherd king.

GOD'S RESCUE

God's great Old Testament rescue points ahead to his greater New Testament rescue.

Adam and Eve turn against God's authority. Sin. It's an attitude of rebellion, which spoils God's world. Sin results in separation from God, and death. But it also leads to broken relationships – Adam blames God and also blames Eve, when he too is guilty (Genesis 3:12). Sin has power over humans and it stains their descendants too.

Enter Abraham! He shows that faith is the path to rescue. He does nothing to deserve God's blessing, but God calls him, and Abraham trusts God by going to the Promised Land. God credits this faith as righteousness (Genesis 15:6) – God sees him as righteous and sinless simply because Abraham believes him.

The Passover shows God's plans for rescue. Israel is trapped in slavery with no sign of escape, until God sends his rescuer, Moses, to bring release. After nine plagues, each family sacrifices a lamb in the place of their firstborn son and spreads its blood on their doors as a sign of their faith in God's rescue. Two things show how God rescues: (1) a substitute takes the blame, and (2) the rescue is for anyone who trusts him, since many others travel with the Israelites (Exodus 12:38). This points ahead to the great New Testament rescue.

God continues rescuing Israel from their enemies when they have trust and faith in him. Joshua, the Judges, Saul, David, and Solomon all see God deliver them from foreign armies. The Canaanites, Philistines, Moabites, and Midianites all feature. Eventually, God hands Israel and Judah over to the Assyrians and Babylonians, before bringing a remnant back home.

The greater New Testament rescue echoes the Passover. The Chosen One is born, and his name, Jesus, means "the Lord saves". He gathers disciples who want their sins forgiven, and goes to the cross to make this rescue possible. (1) He dies as a substitute, carrying God's anger against sin. (2) He rescues any who trust him, including any from foreign nations. The rescue surprises his disciples, who expect a warrior king to defeat the Romans, but his death shows that he is a king that defeats their greatest enemy: sin. Relationships with God and each other can be restored.

New power comes from the Spirit. At Pentecost, the Spirit gives people a double power: power to believe, and power to obey God. He helps the disciples speak in foreign languages and the gospel (good news) spreads like wildfire. Many across the Mediterranean believe, including the Gentiles from all nations.

Jesus makes a threefold rescue. He rescues his people from the penalty of sin (at the cross), from the power of sin (through the Spirit), and from the presence of sin (in the new creation). In the new creation, his rescue is complete and his people triumphantly share his victory, ruling as kings.

THE OLD TESTAMENT

ACT 1: IN THE BEGINNING

Scene 1: VIP Humankind

Humans are the most important part of creation.
God creates the world by speaking: "Let there be… Let there be…" and he loves what he makes. "It's good… It's good!" But at the climax of the sixth day, God makes human beings in his image and tells them to rule over the rest of creation and to increase in number and fill the earth. Now he calls the world "very good".

Scene 2: Living with God

Humans live in harmony with God and creation.
In the Garden of Eden, God rules and humans are responsible vice-rulers. Adam looks for a suitable helper among the animals, naming them all, but none is suitable for him. God makes Eve and they rule happily together. They have a perfect relationship with God, creation, and each other. They live as man and wife.

ACT 2: SPOILED BY SIN

Scene 1: The Fall

Humans reject God and his authority over them.
Adam ("man") and Eve ("mother of all the living") sin by eating the fruit of the tree of the knowledge of good and evil, and fall from their perfect state. All human beings inherit a sinful nature because of them. God banishes them and they will surely die. The Fall results in separation between God and humans, humans and each other, and between humans and the environment.

Scene 2: Sin and Death Spread

Sin leads to death for all human beings.
Disobedience in the Garden escalates to murder and lying, as Cain kills his brother Abel. The curse of death haunts Adam's descendants. In their old age, they die. The people become wicked, violent, and evil, and God sends a flood to recreate the world. But they soon rebel, building the Tower of Babel to be as great as God, and God scatters them. The world needs a rescue.

ACT 3: COVENANTS

Scene 1: God's Promises

God makes four great covenants to give the world hope.
The Noahic Covenant: he promises never again to flood the world. The Abrahamic Covenant: he promises Abraham his own land, countless children and a great nation, and great blessing for them. The Mosaic Covenant: he will make Israel special among the nations. The Davidic Covenant: he will send an eternal king.

Scene 2: The Abrahamic Covenant

God chooses Abraham to be the father of his people.

God promises Abraham countless children, as many as the stars in the sky and the sand on the seashore, and will make them a great nation. He will bless them, and bless anyone who blesses them and curse anyone who curses them. He promises to keep his promises, swearing on his own life. Abraham's nation will know and trust God.

ACT 4: NATION ISRAEL

Scene 1: God's Cast Family

Abraham's family grows and learns of God's faithfulness.

Abraham and Sarah are 100 and 90 respectively when they have Isaac, but God tests Abraham's faith by asking him to give up and kill his son. God spares Isaac and gives him twins: Esau and Jacob. The twins fight, and God chooses Jacob as the next chief. He leads his family to Egypt to live in Goshen, in which Pharaoh lets them live.

Scene 2: God's Rescue

God rescues the Israelite slaves from Egypt.

Pharaoh makes the Israelites (Hebrews) into slaves, who pray for rescue. God meets Moses at a burning bush. God will show Pharaoh who he is. He sends Moses to demand the slaves' release and uses ten plagues to show his supreme power. His people sacrifice a lamb so God can "pass over" their homes, and make an exodus out of Egypt.

Scene 3: God's Special Effects

God blesses his rescued people.

At Mount Sinai, he tells them who they are: they are his rescued people. He treasures them as different and they must live differently. He gives them a law to remember him by, and gives them himself too! He lives among his people in the tabernacle ("the tent of meeting"). Lastly, he gives them sacrifices, which pay for their sins.

Scene 4: God's Location Scout

God's people spy out their fruitful promised land.

Moses sends twelve spies into Canaan to report on their cities, foods, and people. The spies return and spread fear among the people: "The land flows with milk and honey, but we felt like grasshoppers compared to its giants." Joshua and Caleb protest, but Israel ignores them. God sends them to wander in the desert for 40 years.

Scene 5: God's Stage

God hands Canaan over to Joshua and Israel.

The people cross the River Jordan and become a nation. Next is Jericho! The nation circles the city for seven days and God brings down its mighty walls, turning them to rubble. The people act in faith, and God hands Canaan over to them. They work together and God even stops the sun so they can finish a battle in daylight.

Scene 6: God's Judges

Judges lead Israel against its enemies.
After Joshua dies, the people worship foreign idols and God brings foreign armies to rouse them to prayer. There's a cycle of sin, rescue, and sin. They pray and God sends a judge, who beats the enemy, before the people return to the idols. Samson famously kills 1,000 Philistines with a donkey's jawbone, but Israel continues to do whatever it wants.

Scene 7: God's Kings

Kings lead Israel, but few are godly kings.
Israel cries out for a king, against the prophet Samuel's warnings. They anoint Saul, who disobeys God and makes excuses for his sin. Next is David, a man after God's heart. He conquers Israel's enemies and leads Israel to love God. When he sins, he asks for forgiveness. His son Solomon builds the Temple, but turns to foreign gods in his old age.

ACT 5: PROPHETS AND KINGS

Scene 1: Warning and Hope!

Prophets point to God's messages.
They give warnings: Israel must turn from its sin and love God as David had. And they give hope: after a period in exile, they will return home. The kingdom divides and Assyria destroys the northern kingdom of Israel. The southern kingdom of Judah does not learn their lesson, and Babylon conquers and takes them to exile. Jeremiah and Ezekiel's messages go unheeded.

Scene 2: Glimpses of the Messiah

Prophets see the Chosen One coming.
Hope seems lost for Israel and Judah; after all the low points of the Old Testament, how can they live with God and love him faithfully? The prophets foretell a king who will conquer sin and death, who will bless the world and rule for eternity. He will be born in Bethlehem and die for his people's sins. God's people wait for their Messiah…

THE NEW TESTAMENT
ACT 6: THE PROMISED KING

Scene 1: The Son of...

Jesus is born with the right titles.
Matthew calls Jesus the Son of David, the Son of Abraham. He links Jesus to God's promises – Jesus will rule for eternity and bless the world. At Jesus' baptism, God calls him his Son, whom he loves. Jesus is both Immanuel ("God is with us") and the incarnation of God – God in the flesh. The prophets' glimpses come true at his birth.

Scene 2: The Friend of Sinners

Jesus seeks out the trash of society.
Jesus gathers disciples from fishermen, tax collectors, and other "sinners": twelve in all. They are society's outcasts. The religious leaders cannot understand why a religious teacher would eat with those sinners. The difference is that the outcasts know they need a healer, and the religious leaders don't. Jesus comes to forgive sins, and he corrects the Pharisees for their false teaching.

Scene 3: The Man of Superpowers

Jesus shows God's powers.
Jesus claims to forgive sins, and then proves it when he heals the paralysed man. He proves he has power over sin and sickness. He also has God's power over nature: he turns water into wine, calms a storm, and feeds thousands. He has power over death: he raises a dead girl and his friend Lazarus. And he has power over demons and the spirit world.

Scene 4: The Preacher of Parables

Jesus teaches his followers God's ways.
Jesus uses parables to give pictures of God's kingdom and teach people how to treat Jesus as king. He points at everyday things like seeds and nets. He teaches his people to love their enemies, and not to be proud before God. His people must look for forgiveness, and they will find God to be extremely generous like the father in the parable of the Lost Son.

Scene 5: The Servant of Many

Jesus serves his people by dying for them.
The disciples James and John want greatness, but Jesus says it involves service. He says he will die to serve and save his people. He enters Jerusalem on a lowly donkey and many celebrate. But Jesus is charged with blasphemy (claiming to be God) and dies on a cross wearing a crown of thorns. He pays for sins and rises again to prove he has done this.

ACT 7: GLOBAL GOSPEL

Scene 1: Go, Go, Go!

Jesus sends his followers in all directions.
Jesus gathers his disciples and gives them the Great Commission: "Go into all nations and teach them about me." He promises to send his Spirit to help his people with their task, and he ascends to heaven. He sits beside God the Father because his work is done. At Pentecost, the Spirit comes and fills his people with the power to follow Jesus.

Scene 2: New Preachers

The Holy Spirit renews Jesus' followers, who spread the good news.
Sinners find forgiveness and get baptized in order to tell people what they believe: that Jesus has washed their sins away. Peter preaches at Pentecost and 3,000 people believe, and a Pharisee called Saul meets Jesus in a vision. Quickly the Roman world hears the good news about Jesus.

ACT 8: NEW CREATION

Scene 1: Nation Humankind

God gathers his rescued people in the new creation.
John sees a revelation where they wear white robes as forgiven people and worship Jesus on the throne in the city. They come from all nations and languages and wave palm branches in victory. God wipes away every tear from their eyes and there is no longer any death or mourning or crying or pain. It's a new beginning.

Scene 2: God's New Eden

The people live forever in paradise.
In the new Eden, the river of the water of life and the tree of life give eternal life. There is no longer any curse, and God's rescued people reign with Jesus as kings. Before this can happen, Jesus promises to return to judge humanity. He calls himself the bright morning star. A morning star signals dawn, and Jesus comes to signal the eternal dawn.

ACTING IN LESSONS

Want to have fun *and* make progress? Acting can be the greatest thing to do in RE lessons. It's challenging, it aids memory, and it is thoroughly skills-based.

VALUES

Involve all children

Give everyone a role! Try splitting into groups, or increasing the number of cast and crew, or giving rewards to build competition.

Focus on creative skills

Avoid a bland recitation of lines. Watch clips online for acting tips. Use peer review to help the children be the leaders. If it gets stale, call "cut!".

Grow teamwork and listening skills

Allocate roles and avoid stepping in on every mistake, but let the acting continue. Mistakes can be the best teacher.

TIMING

Plan time generously

Allow time for going through roles, learning parts, rehearsing, performing, reviewing, re-performing and filming, and watching back.

Plan ahead

Choose a couple of acting exercises and help the students get good at them. It saves on explanation time. Allocate roles ahead so children can prepare costumes and props.

Get it going

GIG! Allocate rough space and locations. Avoid too much speaking – it's the children's show!

KIT

Props and costumes

Collect multipurpose items: staffs and sticks, cloaks or dressing gowns (brown, white, blue), and wigs! Grow a props box and ask the children to donate.

Camera

Find one with "plug and play" or a big screen so everyone can watch it straight back. If in school, check the policy if permission is needed. Encourage the children to film only when it's good enough. Avoid the zoom!

Clapperboard

The child director writes on and uses the clapperboard. They begin the scene and also give feedback.

Microphone

Use for group interviews. Lift up a microphone to show who is allowed to speak, or pass around a microphone to show the designated speaker.

Backing music

Encourage students to think about the tone of the scene: seriousness/speed/sounds. Ask the music department for instruments, or play a movie score on a computer.

Awards statuettes

Generate competition – see more opposite on Reviewing.

SET LINGO

"Quiet on set!"
The teacher signals the start with silence.

"Lights, Camera, Action!"
When ready to perform, quieten the students for a proper start.

"Background action!"
When filming, this tells the minor parts to get moving, before the main characters do their thing.

"Cut!"
Call a stop if something really must be changed, or when the scene is finished.

"Scene... Take 3!"
The clapperboard holder introduces the big idea again. Try a strict limit to the number of takes.

"It's a wrap, people!"
The final cut is good. Pack up the set and watch the final cut if filmed.

VARIETY

There are many acting exercises in The Teacher's Cut. Use a few, but not too many – the children should get familiar and good at them.

Cast and crew
Involve many children all at once. Allocate key roles first – main characters, director, scriptwriter – and then choose remaining cast and crew members. Perform a scene in the middle of the room and then give the crew their chance to review it. You can also hand out photocopiable role sheets (p. 115). Actors' understudies can swap in for the characters when it's time for a change. Replay a scene multiple times until it's excellent, or filmable.

Acting groups
Build competition by getting more than one group to perform a scene. Reward key performance with statuettes. Or divide a long act into different scenes and allocate the scenes to different groups. Display the scene list and then perform them back-to-back. This works well with the life of Moses, for example.

Hot seating
This is a classic method of acting in lessons. Choose one or two children to perform as characters and get them to stand/sit at the front. Play out the feeling between them (how do they feel about each other?), and interview them. Reward thoughtful questions and answers. Great questions often begin with why or how, but less what.

Object drama
If technology and time allows, try stop-motion animation. Set up a camera and some models, play dough, or Lego, and take pictures of the actions. Record a voiceover for the narrator and characters. Or try using finger puppets. Put a table on its end and perform the scene from behind it. The children (at home or in the Art Department) could make puppets.

Mime artists
Cut out the dialogue and perform through poses. Allocate a stage area (perhaps mark it with masking tape) and replay a scene with big gestures and emotion. Or use still poses. List a number of pictures you want or use the photocopiable role sheets (p. 88, 119, 125), and cast the performance. Play the director and take pictures from the same position.

REVIEWING

Leave time to watch the movie or discuss learning points. Keep books open to read key lines and actions and discuss the meaning. Discuss the shock or surprise in the scene.

Have an awards ceremony such as The Galilee Globes. Use categories: Best Actor, Best Actress, Best Supporting, Best Crew Member. Use awards music and play-off music for long speeches.

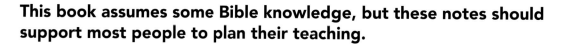

GUIDE TO PRODUCTION NOTES

This book assumes some Bible knowledge, but these notes should support most people to plan their teaching.

UNIT AIM

This comes out of the scene card. Bear it in mind when picking which texts to cover in your course – ensure that your selection teaches the aim.

UNIT CONTENT

This is a rough outline of the topics in *The Blockbuster Bible*. These also form a sort of "checklist" for the teacher to cover.

SCENE CARD

This summary explains the scene of the story. It uses keywords that the children are expected to know how to use. One suggestion is to create a slideshow of the scene cards and challenge children to explain fully what the scene is about.

WIDE ANGLE: SETTING THE SCENE

This is the essential reading for the Bible background. Paragraph one gives the wider view, and paragraph two zooms in a little.

CLOSE-UP

One story may carry the teaching of the scene more directly. The close-up unpacks this key story to help you spot more of what's happening in the text.

FLASH-FORWARD/FLASHBACK

All good stories carry suggestions of the past or future. The Bible is packed with little pointers to linked events. Promise and fulfilment are key ideas and children should make the connections.

BONUS FEATURES

This is some information that might interest the children. They are modern-day facts or ideas, and trivia nuggets to unpack the passages.

GUIDE TO ACTION PLANS

This is a menu of activities, not a recipe! Plan your lessons in your own way, but these activities and sheets may help.

SCENE CARD

Use the scene cards for discussion and writing tasks. Use the word bank to write a three to four line summary in the back of exercise books or a set-aside space. Use the Glossary in *The Blockbuster Bible* for some meanings.

CONCEPT ACTIVITY

Get the children active and thinking about the ideas on the unit. These often need equipment, so plan ahead.

GAMES

Bring some fun and competition to your lessons with some quizzes, new games, and some old classics.

CLIPS

Introduce a story or prepare for acting exercises! Always check a video before showing it, and say what to look out for. Good starting places: *What's in the Bible* DVDs (13–part series); *The Bible Project* (on YouTube).

SHEETS

Use the photocopiable sheets related to each topic. Many of them are explained in the Action Plans. Particularly watch out for FLEXI-TASKS, which are non-topic specific. They are left wide open for you to use in any unit or task. This does mean, however, that the children may need more help getting started with them.

MODELLING

Get some play dough (or plasticine) for the odd modelling activity. See Perfect Models (in "VIP Humankind"), or Build a Tabernacle (in "God's Special Effects").

MUSIC

Support the tone of a story by listening to some background music as you read.

READING/RESEARCH

Go further with some extension reading or research online, or use the text provided here to give you some pointers.

ACTING

Role play and drama is a large part of this resource. Use the guide to acting on pages 16–17, and enjoy the different options available!

SPECIAL FEATURES
THE MAKING OF THE BIBLE

PRODUCTION NOTES

UNIT AIM

- *To understand the making of the Bible*

UNIT CONTENT

- *Who wrote the Bible and when*
- *Bible writing styles*
- *Timeline of the Bible story*
- *Languages involved*

WIDE ANGLE: SETTING THE SCENE

The Bible comes in two halves: the Old Testament and the New Testament. Testament means "agreement between God and his people". In the Old Testament, God agrees to make his people special and different. In the New Testament, God does this through his Son Jesus.

About 40 authors wrote the Bible over 1,600 years, but the oldest stories were first told in the oral tradition many years before. The Bible writers state that it is inspired by God (2 Timothy 3:16). The writers used different writing styles. Law: The Five Books of Moses are the Jewish Torah (or Pentateuch). Genesis, Exodus, Leviticus, Numbers, and Deuteronomy show how God establishes Israel and shows them how to live. History: These books show Israel's history under Joshua, David, and other kings. Poetry: David wrote many of the Psalms and, according to tradition, Solomon wrote Ecclesiastes. Over one third of the Bible is poetry. Prophets: These books contain messages of warning and hope to Israel and Judah. They also point further into the future toward the Messiah. Gospels: Four books recording Jesus' life, death, and resurrection. Letters: Jesus' disciples explained how to trust and obey Jesus. Revelation: John's vision of Jesus' rule over all things and of the new creation, where Jesus gathers his chosen people.

CLOSE-UP

The 2 Testaments are 2 agreements between God and his people. They have faith, and he provides. In the Old Testament, Israel trusts and obeys him to make them special (the Mosaic Covenant). But Israel fails again and again! In the New Testament, Jesus' followers trust that he has paid for their sins (the New Covenant). The bread and wine are rescue reminders for them.

The Law is often called the Pentateuch or the Torah. It is the 5 books written by Moses to guide God's people. Torah means "instruction", since it includes the Ten Commandments and the 613 laws to God's people.

BONUS FEATURES ✪✪✪

Did you know?

- *The Bible has always been popular and copied carefully. The 25,000 handwritten manuscripts that survive from the ancient world were used until the invention of the printing press. The Bible was also the first mass-produced book in Europe.*

- *The Bible isn't the oldest book around today. The oldest machine-printed book is the 15th-century Gutenberg Bible, but one of the oldest surviving books is an Etruscan script written around 2,500 years ago. It was found in a tomb in Bulgaria and is 6 pages of undeciphered script written on 24-carat gold tablets.*

ACTION PLANS

BIBLE HOT SEATING

Perform as and interview the Bible on its making.

Choose a child to "play" the Bible, talking about the Bible in the first person. Invite open-ended questions from the students that hint at learned material. Everyone should practise using the key facts and statistics related to the making of the Bible. They should be quite confident conversationalists in order to keep up the charade and discussion. They may also hold a Bible as a helpful prop. Keep the exercise sensible – the child shouldn't ham up the performance too much, and other children shouldn't comment on the quality of the discussion, but they can only ask further questions. All must enter into the spirit of it. Rotate the child playing the Bible.

MEMORY-MAKING

Test the students on the key facts of the making of the Bible.

Give 2 minutes for the children to look up the key facts and statistics in the chapter. They then close books and the teacher writes their memorized facts on the board. Add any missing. Give them one minute to remember the list. Then rub all (or parts) off the board and test them again.

Alternatively, the children can write their memorized facts in their books. You could also play a game of quick-fire rounds. How quickly can the students recall all the facts, with no one speaking more than once? Time them to give you all the main facts, having rubbed them off the board.

Note facts to look for: number of authors, languages, years to write; dates range; testaments; number of books and types of writing; meanings of types of writing.

PASSAGE LOOKUP

Consider what the Bible says about its making.

Who wrote the Bible? How can about 40 authors all produce one story? Read 2 Timothy 3:16. What does "God-breathed" mean?

CLIP

Explore the literary styles in the Bible

On YouTube search "The Bible Project: Literary Styles in the Bible" (5:27mins). Discuss the key ideas and list the types of writing.

Sheet: Grouping Facts

Categorize the Bible's facts and statistics.

Use the sheet Grouping Facts to categorize information about the Bible. Get the children to work out the groupings, or give them these ideas: numbers, books, number of books, types of writing, names. Help children to lay out the cards neatly and avoid piling them up. Challenge them to explain their groupings and write words under the numbers.

Variation: the children could come up with their own facts, names, and statistics and group them accordingly. Work as individuals, pairs, or groups.

FLEXI-TASK

Sheet: Trivia Cards

Make quiz cards on Bible facts.

Use the Trivia Cards page to make your own quiz. E.g. Category: Old Testament. Questions: How many books are there in the Old Testament? What are the 4 types of Old Testament books? Give 2 more facts about the Old Testament.

FLEXI-TASK

SPECIAL FEATURES
THE BIG STORY OF THE BIBLE

PRODUCTION NOTES

UNIT AIM

- To summarize the whole Bible story

UNIT CONTENT

- Summaries of 4 popular children's stories
- Three themes of the Bible story
- Selected highlights of the Bible story

WIDE ANGLE: SETTING THE SCENE

The Bible's central character is God, so it's easiest to tell the story with God as the main focus. There are 3 themes that sum it up quite nicely: *Living with God, God's Promises, God's Rescue*. Each theme runs right through the Bible story.

Living with God is about God's relationship with his people. The story begins in the Garden of Eden, where God lives with humans in harmony. Soon sin spoils the relationship and God banishes them from his presence. He comes to live with his people in the tabernacle ("tent of meeting") in the desert. The Temple of Jerusalem later replaces the tabernacle. In the New Testament, God "tabernacles" with his people – Jesus lives among them. He sends his Spirit to live within all believers, and eventually brings them to live with him in the new creation.

God's Promises is about how God fulfils his promises, most notably those to Eve, Abraham, and David. God promises Eve a snake crusher from her descendants – someone to defeat sin and death. God promises Abraham land, children, and blessing – one of his descendants will bless the world. God promises David a descendant to rule for eternity. Jesus fulfils these on the cross and in the new creation.

God's Rescue is about how God deals with his people's biggest problem: their sin. They reject God's authority. The attitude of sin causes separation from God, so God plans to pay for their sin and live with them again.

CLOSE-UP

Sin is how people turn their backs on God and his rule. It's an attitude, not just an action. Sin leads to death, and the 3 themes of the Bible revolve around how God overcomes the problem. He wants to (1) live with his people, so he (2) promises to defeat sin, and (3) sends Jesus to rescue his people.

BONUS FEATURES ✪✪✪

Did you know?

- *Bible characters make for great movies. Hollywood often uses characters like Moses for big-budget features, but the most viewed movie in history is about Jesus. Jesus has been translated into 1,700 languages and apparently viewed over 8 billion times.*

ACTION PLANS

SEVEN-WORD STORIES

Summarize the Bible story in 7 words.

Think about a famous story: e.g. Little Red Riding Hood, Peter Pan, Robin Hood, The Lion, the Witch and the Wardrobe. Describe the beginning, middle, and end. What makes you care about the story? How do you set the scene?

Summarize these in 7 words, stating the characters, enemies, location, and simple plot. "Outlaw saves Maid Marian from selfish sheriff." YouTube has some very funny clips on stories in 5 seconds.

Cover the 3 themes of the Bible Story – Living with God, God's Promises, God's Rescue. Summarize a theme in 7 words.

THE CONFIDENCE WALL

Test familiarity with the Bible.

Explain the "confidence wall". It is one wall of the room where "know-it-alls" stand at one end and "not-at-all-sures" stand at the other. Pose a series of questions and select students for testing: what is a testament? What is sin? Who was Abraham? Tell the Bible story in 7 words.

Alternatively, place them on the "knowledge line". Test them on their Bible knowledge – they move up or down depending on their answers. Start easy, and choose children at random. Or test on where something fits into the story – God, sin, the Israelites, Jesus, heaven.

CLIP

Explore the story of the Bible.

On YouTube search "The Bible Project: The Story of the Bible" (5:37mins). Discuss the key ideas and explain the 3 themes in the book.

TEASER POSTER

Design a poster on a theme of the Bible story, imagining it as a movie.

Look at some teaser posters online and consider the features (tag line, title, cast/characters). Design a poster on a theme of the Bible story: Living with God, God's Promises, God's Rescue.

FLEXI-TASK

Sheet: Complete the Clapperboard

Map out the key details and story of a scene in the Bible

Look at Popcorn Sally's selected highlights on page 9 of *The Blockbuster Bible*.

Choose a story and fill in the clapperboard and production notes on the key moment of that scene, and why it's important.
Or try using the page as a starter activity for another story.

FLEXI-TASK

ACT 1: IN THE BEGINNING
SCENE 1: VIP HUMANKIND

PRODUCTION NOTES

UNIT AIM

- *To see why humankind is very important*

UNIT CONTENT

- *God makes the world in 7 days*
- *Reasons why humans are very important*

WIDE ANGLE: SETTING THE SCENE

God makes humans VIPs – Very Important People! The whole story leads up to God making them at the climax of day 6. Until then, he calls everything "good", but after he makes them, he calls the world "very good". He makes them "in his image" (see Close-up) and blesses them to rule over the earth and fill it. VIP humankind is different from the animals, and is the crowning achievement of God's creation.

The creation story paints a picture about power. God is the creator who speaks to create. When he says *"Let there be light!"*, light appears. When he calls for land, there's land. But God also makes humans and gives power to them. He tells them to rule over the creation and increase over the face of the earth. God is the creator and humans are the stewards. They rule with power under God's higher rule.

SCENE CARD

Red Carpet: God creates VIP Humankind in his image and tells them to fill and rule the world.

CLOSE-UP

God makes humankind *"in his image"* (Genesis 1:26–27). This means that they will follow God's example as the world's ruler and be capable of relationships.

Blessing means that God favours humankind. It's a special happiness with and from God. He blesses them to fulfil their role as rulers under him (Genesis 1:28).

FLASH-FORWARD >>>

Curse is the opposite of blessing. While work is a blessing at creation, work will become very hard after sin corrupts humankind (Genesis 3:17–19).

BONUS FEATURES ✪✪✪

Did you know?

- *Genesis 1 contains Hebrew poetic features. For example, the days parallel each other. In days 1-3 God makes habitats, and he fills them in days 4-6. Also there are repeated phrases like "let there be", "and it was so", "there was evening and there was morning".*

ACTION PLANS

SCENE CARD

Red Carpet: Consider how God makes humans most important.

PRESENT RED CARPET.

- *What's a red carpet for?*
- *What is the most important species on earth?*
- *Why might humans be the most important?*

Word bank for 3–4 line summary:
God, humans, important, image, rule, increase, very good.

PERFECT MODELS

Consider how it feels to create and call our creation "good" or "very good".
Hand out some play dough and give the children 5 minutes to design an animal. Emphasize the need to care about the design and detail. Afterward, review what it was like to make these and what makes the models "good" or "very good".

Alternatively, save this activity for The Fall (two units' time), when you can destroy them to illustrate the effect of sin on friendships.

MOOD MUSIC

Stir the senses while reading the creation story.
Play some music from YouTube, perhaps from a soundtrack like *The Lord of the Rings*, or from *The Planets – Mars*, by Holst. Allocate readers before beginning to read and then let the mood take over.

MIDDLE OF THE WORLD

Share opinions by voting with your feet.
Place a bullseye in the middle of the room, which stands for the middle of the world. A child should stand there and make a statement that others may agree/disagree with, e.g. "humankind was the best bit of creation". Children stand according to their strength of opinion – close if they agree, far if they disagree. Have the children explain their position and question each other.

THE MAGICIAN'S NEPHEW

Consider the links between the creation stories in C. S. Lewis's Narnia and the Bible.
Read out some quotes from *The Magician's Nephew* (1955) in the chapter "The Founding of Narnia". Aslan, the lion king of the land of Narnia, sings and speaks to create the world. Discuss why the children think C. S. Lewis used the Bible's creation story for the creation of Narnia. (N.B. Lewis believed the Bible, and used Narnia as a picture of the world.)

> *The second wonder was that the blackness overhead, all at once, was blazing with stars.… One moment there had been nothing but darkness; next moment a thousand, thousand points of light leaped out - single stars, constellations, and planets, brighter and bigger than any in our world.… it was the First Voice, the deep one, which had made them appear and made them sing.*

What does Lewis call the creator? How is he like the creator in the Bible?

> *The Lion… stared at the animals… And gradually a change came over them. The smaller ones - the rabbits, moles and such-like - grew a good deal larger. The very big ones - you noticed it most with the elephants - grew a little smaller… the deepest, wildest voice they had ever heard was saying: "Narnia, Narnia, Narnia, awake. Love. Think. Speak. Be walking trees. Be talking beasts. Be divine waters."*

What does Aslan do to create?

When you listened to Aslan's song you heard the things he was making up: when you looked around you, you saw them.

What would it be like to watch Aslan create?

Sheet: VIP Card

Make a VIP card for humankind.

Sheet: Acceptance Speech

Write an acceptance speech for VIP Humankind.

Use the blueprint and VIP card in *The Blockbuster Bible* to include as many keywords and ideas as possible.

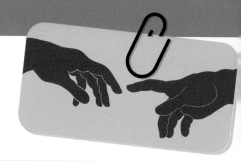

ACT 1: IN THE BEGINNING
SCENE 2: LIVING WITH GOD

PRODUCTION NOTES

UNIT AIM

- *To understand why God makes humans*

UNIT CONTENT

- *God makes the Garden of Eden and humans*
- *God gives Adam a job and free will*
- *God makes helpers for Adam*

WIDE ANGLE: SETTING THE SCENE

VIP Humankind's biggest blessing is living with God. God makes them to live with him in the Garden of Eden – Eden means "delight". Adam and Eve are delighted to live with God because they are living the life they were made to live. They rule the Garden well together, and God walks in the Garden too. Living with God means total harmony – perfect relationships with God, with each other, and with the creation itself. There's no guilt, shame, blame, or embarrassment. And the animals are safe to be with! The rest of the Bible story shows how humans live with God (and how they don't!).

God gives Adam and Eve great responsibility, and the rest of the Bible story shows how people use it. They need to rule the creation together. In Eden Adam names the animals, and even names himself (Adam means "humankind"). God gives one rule: they cannot eat from the tree of the knowledge of good and evil. If they do, God promises they will die.

SCENE CARD

Two Hands: God lives in Eden with humans and tells them not to eat from a particular tree.

CLOSE-UP

Harmony marks out humankind's 3 relationships. It means to "get on well". An orchestra harmonizes well when its various parts combine to produce a beautiful sound. Humankind, God, and nature will combine to produce a beautiful world, so long as humankind fulfils its role.

FLASH-FORWARD >>>

Genesis 2 subtly hints at what is ahead. God forbids eating from the tree (2:17). He promises that man will otherwise die (2:17). Adam and his wife were naked and felt no shame (2:25). Soon humankind will choose to disobey, and shame will follow where there was none before.

BONUS FEATURES ✪✪✪

Did you know?

- *Hebrew words show the close relationship between God and humans. God forms the man from the dust of the ground. The word for "formed" is yatsar, like how a potter forms clay. Man and the ground are also closely linked - adam and adamah are used respectively.*

- *The Garden is pictured like a divine sanctuary. Hebrew words for "work" and "keep" are also used for priests who "minister" and "serve" in the tabernacle later in the Old Testament. Adam's role is to be not only a gardener but also a guardian. He is to maintain the holiness of the Garden just like a temple complex.*

ACTION PLANS

SCENE CARD

Two Hands: Consider how God designs humans to live with him.

PRESENT TWO HANDS.

- *Who are these characters?*
- *How do they feel about each other?*
- *How much is life like that today?*

Word bank for 3–4 line summary:
Adam, Eden, living, helper, rule, woman, free will.

MAN OR ROBOT?

Play a blindfolded game showing how choice helps friendships.

Discuss why God made the tree of the knowledge of good and evil. Is it good or bad? How does choice help friendships?

Have the children close their eyes and tap some to be robots – they must obey your instructions. The others are human – they can choose! Open eyes and follow instructions: e.g. do 3 press-ups, do a group goal celebration, shake someone's hand, salute the teacher, compliment someone. Discuss the choices they made. What did it feel like when people choose to obey? Why is the tree of the knowledge of good and evil a good thing?

ANIMAL NAMES

Research the origins of some animal names.

Go online and see how some animals got their names. Search the etymology of hippopotamus, octopus, panther (panthera), lynx, giraffe. Discuss how we name things and link to Adam naming the animals.

HARMONY HOT SEATING

Interview Adam and Eve on their harmonious lives.

Present and discuss these words: harmony, free will, choice, rule, blessing, friendships. Cast children to play Adam and Eve. They sit at the front. The rest of the students interview them on the selected words. Start off the questioning: why is the Garden of Eden a place of harmony?

Ask open-ended questions – starting with what/how/why, is/does. Questions cannot relate to sin/evil because Adam and Eve won't understand! Rotate who plays Adam and Eve.

RELATIONSHIPS RADIO PLAY

Write a conversation between Adam, Eve, and God to show the harmony in creation.

Discuss how to write a radio play. Stage directions and sound effects are written in square brackets. E.g. start by writing that God is walking in the Garden. Afterward, 3 children perform the radio play; others can provide the sound effects (when appropriate). Just focus on the story before the snake and eating the fruit.

Sheet: Blueprinting

Create a blueprint design of the Garden of Eden using the pictures, cut out and stuck onto graph paper.

Sheet: Adam's Friendships

Write friendship statuses for Adam.

Imagine you are Adam and write friendship statuses to describe what happened between you, God, the animals, and Eve. Carefully follow the action in *The Blockbuster Bible*.

ACT 2: SPOILED BY SIN
SCENE 1: THE FALL

PRODUCTION NOTES

UNIT AIM

- *To see how sin spoils friendship with God*

UNIT CONTENT

- *Adam and Eve disobey God*
- *God's punishments*

WIDE ANGLE: SETTING THE SCENE

Adam and Eve misuse their responsibility and sin. Sin is rejection of God's authority. It's saying, "Shove off, God, I'm in charge. No to your rules!" The snake (who stands for the devil) tempts and lies to Eve, telling her that she will not die but instead be like God, knowing good and evil. The thing is, she's already like God, made in his image! Now she wants to take his place. Eve recounts God's rule and eats the fruit anyway – rejection of God's authority. Adam is there too and he also chooses to eat it. They are both guilty.

God's punishments show what human life will be like. Relationships with God, with each other, and with the creation itself are all spoiled. Adam blames Eve, who blames the serpent. Adam even blames God. This is the beginning of the "sinful nature" – all humans are "fallen". In the New Testament, Paul says humans are "slaves to sin" (Romans 6:6). Since the Fall, humans cannot help rejecting God's authority. And sin leads to separation from God, and eventually death. God gives hope by promising to send a snake crusher – someone to defeat sin and death. This person will defeat the devil, but die in the process. Jesus completes this mission on the cross, and gathers his people to live in the new creation, a world without sin and death.

SCENE CARD

Back Turned: Humans believe the snake's lies and turn against the rule of God, who banishes them.

CLOSE-UP

Sin stains God's people for the rest of the Bible story. Humans now need *God's Rescue*. Sin spoils their relationships with God, with each other, and with creation itself. And sin leads to death. *Living with God* is not possible because God is holy – he is separate from sin and must banish them. But *God's Promises* begin here – he will send a snake crusher to defeat sin and death.

Grace accompanies judgment. God gives an undeserved gift: he makes Adam and Eve clothes from animal skins to hide their shame. Sin stains humans, but grace helps them. See also Scene 2!

FLASH-FORWARD >>>

God promises that Eve's offspring will crush the snake's head, but the snake will strike his heel (Genesis 3:15). The singular "he" and "his" suggests one particular person ("offspring"). The New Testament presents this snake-crusher offspring as Jesus, who will overcome Satan at the cross, but be killed at the same time (Hebrews 2:14).

BONUS FEATURES ✪✪✪
Did you know?

- *Adam and Eve eat a fruit from the tree of the knowledge of good and evil, not specifically an apple!*

ACTION PLANS

SCENE CARD

Back Turned: Consider how humankind turns their back on God and each other.

PRESENT BACK TURNED.

- *How do we feel when someone does this to us?*
- *Who might we do this to?*
- *Who was the last one Adam and Eve have done this to?*

Word bank for 3–4 line summary:
snake, lie, fruit, sin, punish, death, banish.

ENTERING ENEMIES

Consider how enemies affect stories.

Quiz the students on famous enemies by naming stories: e.g. Robin Hood, Peter Pan, *Star Wars*, Harry Potter, *The Lord of the Rings*, Batman, Spider-Man, Superman. Who are the worst, and why? How are they introduced in movies – is there scary music, a rising camera angle?

Who is the enemy in the Bible story? How is he pictured, and why? What does he cause to happen? How can he be "beaten"? (Draw out how the devil brings sin, and how God must rescue humankind from sin.)

TOOTHPASTE SQUIRTING

Consider how decisions can be messy and can't be taken back.

Equipment: *Toothpaste, coloured paper, and wet tissues/cloths for cleaning hands.*

Discuss good and bad decisions, and mistakes. How do we fix mistakes? Show a toothpaste tube and coloured paper and tell two children to paint a house on the paper. The toothpaste represents our actions and words each day. How can the painters change something (sometimes it's not possible)? Tell the painters to put the toothpaste back in the tube.

Link to Adam and Eve's mistake, and how they couldn't take it back. This activity can also be done with a hammer, wood, and nails to represent how holes can't be removed, like humankind's wrong actions and words.

Sheet: Fixing the Fall

Cut out and fix a puzzle of pictures about the Fall.

Sheet: Storyboarding the Fall

Complete a storyboard of the events of the Fall.

SPOILING MODELS

Build and smash play dough models to show how humankind spoiled God's world.

Equipment: *Play dough/modelling clay, hammer!*

Children design an animal in 3 minutes. Emphasize the care for detail (or bring the models out of the cupboard if they made them earlier). Discuss how the world today isn't perfect, and how Christians believe there was a day when the world "fell" from its perfect state. Without warning (and children must stand back), hammer them flat, or have children smash their friend's one. Use discretion! Link to sin and its impact on harmony.

CLIP

Explore the meaning of sin.

On YouTube search "The Bible Project: Word Study: Khata – 'Sin'" (5:42mins). Discuss the key ideas.

WRITE A MOVIE SCRIPT

Write and perform a movie script for the Fall.

Use the storyboard in this book to write a movie script: 1 line of speech for each picture. Children write 1–10 down one side of their page (leaving 2 lines' gap between each). Then write dramatic speech to accompany each picture. Include the emotions they considered in Entering Enemies, Toothpaste Squirting, or Spoiling Models. Children then perform their script as others follow the drama on the storyboard again.

ACTING

Perform the Fall as a group or series of mini plays.

Cast: Eve, the snake, Adam, God, two angels. Briefly recap the story and remind of the tone and feeling of the drama. Give everyone a few moments in silence to learn their parts and then get together to share their ideas. Then let the action commence! Film it if there's time to watch it back.

ACT 2: SPOILED BY SIN
SCENE 2: SIN AND DEATH SPREAD

PRODUCTION NOTES

UNIT AIM

- *To see how sin worsens God's world*

UNIT CONTENT

- *Cain murders his brother Abel*
- *Adam's descendants die*
- *Violence and the flood*
- *Rebellion and the Tower of Babel*

WIDE ANGLE: SETTING THE SCENE

Sin stains Adam and Eve's descendants too. Their son Cain murders his brother Abel, even after God warns him to be careful. God also banishes him further east, the same direction Adam and Eve were sent from Eden. And sin always leads to death – Genesis 5 lists many of Adam's descendants dying: "He died… and he died… and he died." By Genesis 6, the people are corrupt, violent, and wicked. Their thoughts are only evil all the time. It seems no one can escape this terrible condition; even after God's flood, which he sends to recreate the world, the builders of the Tower of Babel want to be as great as God. Sin and death spread right through God's world as he sends them further east.

There is still hope! God shows his grace (undeserved generosity) in each episode. He marks Cain to protect him after he kills his brother. He spares Enoch from the taste of death because Enoch walks in friendship with him for 300 years. He spares Noah and his family from the flood and promises never to send one again. None of these people were perfect – none deserved God's generosity. This nicely leads up to Abraham. Abraham is not perfect either, but God will change history through his family.

SCENE CARD

Gravestones: Sin worsens in murder, violence, and rebellion, and the punishment for sin is death.

CLOSE-UP

Judgment continues… It is how God deals with sin. Sometimes it involves punishment, such as wiping out the world, and sometimes it involves stopping a problem continue, such as scattering the people of the world.

Grace continues… God follows up judgment with undeserved gifts. He protects Cain with a mark. He takes Enoch away before his death. He saves Noah and his family from the flood. None deserve it.

FLASH-FORWARD >>>

God's grace to Enoch and Noah hints at a hopeful future where God removes his judgment from sinful people. Though they were still sinful, God saved them from death. In the New Testament, God removes his judgment from humankind as Jesus dies on their behalf. Though death comes to all, in the end it loses its sting (1 Corinthians 15:55).

BONUS FEATURES ✪✪✪

Did you know?

- *Adam and his descendants still lived for many years. Adam died aged 930, his son Seth died at 912, and his son Enosh died at 905. The point is still clear - everyone dies in the end. Later, God shortens humans' lives to 120 years (Genesis 6:3).*
- *Babel is a verb meaning "to confuse, to mix to mingle". This is also the name used in the Old Testament for the city of Babylon, which symbolizes humankind's ambition to dethrone God and rule earth alone.*

ACTION PLANS

SCENE CARD

Gravestones: Consider how sin leads to death.

PRESENT GRAVESTONES.

- *Why is this a sad picture?*
- *Why do humans die? What did God say?*
- *How might people sin today?*

Word bank for 3-4 line summary:
sin, spreads, murder, violence, rebellion, punishment, death

ROTTING FRUIT

Explore how rot spreads between fruit.

Equipment: *Apples and time!*
Explore how rot spreads between fruit. Look at photos online (search: "rot spreads fruit") or bring in some rotting fruit. Often rot spreads through contact, so bring a pair of apples that share a rotten side.

   Discuss how bad decisions can lead to more bad decisions. People lie and lie more to cover it up. Or people hurt and retaliate. Or people are told off and then react badly and are told off more. How did Adam and Eve sin? What would it cause? Link this to their children and sin spread in murder, death, violence, and rebellion. Are these mistakes inevitable, or can they be helped?

Sheet: Sin and Death Spread

Find how sin spreads like rot.

Hand out the sheets and discuss sin, punishment, and grace. Why does sin lead to punishment? What is grace (undeserved generosity)? The children should use the storyboards in *The Blockbuster Bible* to complete the table.

   Variation: sort the sin, judgment, and grace into these 3 categories and rank them in size order – which is the greatest sin/judgment/grace, etc.? Then try re-ranking them in surprise order – which is most surprising? Then perhaps include the Fall – does that change the orders?

STUDENT COLLABORATION

Work together to design a fantastic storyboard.

Children work in pairs. Each pair has 5 minutes to start a storyboard, then passes it on. Children keep adding, and can rub out incorrect/unclear work. Keep rotating work until the task has had its time. Return the work to its original owners, who compare it to their original vision or idea.
   Try this with:

- *Writing scripts for 4 storyboards*
- *Writing a diary for one character in a storyboard*
- *Drawing the main scene from a storyboard*
- *Drawing a series of new images as a new storyboard*

FLEXI-TASK

Sheet: Storyboarding

Design a storyboard on an episode.

Discuss how storyboards show film-makers how to film a scene. Each picture needs a title and speech. Consider different types of shots – wide angles, close-ups, zoom-ins, and panning shots (moving across). Make one storyboard for the 4 stories of Sin and Death Spreads, or choose one scene.

ACT 3: COVENANTS
SCENE 1: GOD'S PROMISES

PRODUCTION NOTES

UNIT AIM

- *To see how promises change the Bible story*

UNIT CONTENT

- *Promises and reminders*
- *The Noahic Covenant*
- *The Abrahamic Covenant*
- *The Mosaic Covenant*
- *The Davidic Covenant*

WIDE ANGLE: SETTING THE SCENE

God's covenants change the direction of the Bible story. God is a covenant-making God – he makes agreements with his people and intends to rescue people to live with him again. It's clear that God is committed to these covenants, as he marks them with reminders.

God promises Noah, the animals, and all future generations that he will never send another flood to wipe out the world. He points at a rainbow to remind them – a sign of peace after the storm. Out of the blue, God promises to give Abraham land, children, and blessing – and one of his descendants will bless the world. The New Testament begins by calling Jesus the Son of Abraham. God marks this promise with circumcision – Abraham and his nation must mark their bodies to remember God's plan. Later at Mount Sinai, God agrees to make Israel special among the nations if they obey him. The sabbath will remind them that they are different, as they rest on the 7th day of each week.

Much later, God promises David that his throne and kingdom will last forever – a descendant of David will rule his people for eternity. This covenant doesn't come with a reminder, but God is still committed. The New Testament begins by also calling Jesus the Son of David. God's promises show the way ahead for his people.

SCENE CARD

Wedding Rings: God makes promises to help his people, like Noah, Abraham, Israel, and David.

CLOSE-UP

Covenant means a long-lasting agreement between God and his people. Each one is a binding agreement. God will not abandon his people to their sin. Sometimes they are unilateral (God unconditionally promises never again to destroy the world with a flood); sometimes they are bilateral (God expects his people to obey him through the Old Testament laws and commandments).

FLASH-FORWARD >>>

The first 3 covenants pave the way for the Davidic Covenant. There, God promises King David that one of his descendants will be a king to rule forever, into eternity (2 Samuel 7:13–14). The New Testament says the "Son of David" is Jesus (Matthew 1:1). This unconditional covenant will affect humankind more than the previous 3 covenants studied here.

BONUS FEATURES ✪✪✪

Did you know?

- *"Covenant" appears 285 times in the Old Testament and 33 in the New Testament. It is one of the most important concepts in the Bible, and the word "testament" is even another name for covenant.*

ACTION PLANS

SCENE CARD

Wedding Rings: Consider how God makes promises to fix his world.

PRESENT WEDDING RINGS.

- *What are wedding rings for?*
- *Why is it important to remember promises?*
- *Will they go away if we forget them?*

Word bank for 3-4 line summary:
promises, covenants, reminders, Noahic, Abrahamic, Mosaic, Davidic.

STORY STRUCTURES

Consider how storylines often work.

Discuss what happens in stories: beginning/middle/ends. Discuss problems that appear in these stories: Robin Hood, Peter Pan, Cinderella, Little Red Riding Hood.

Link to the problem in the Bible story (sin and death). Discuss God's promises to fix the problem, and why we follow these for the rest of the story.

Sheet: Covenant Categories

Look up details on 4 of God's Covenants.

Use the sheet provided (with some squares already filled in), or draw up a 5x4 square table on the whiteboard for the children to copy. Write the names of the covenants down the first column (leave the top-left square blank). Write these headings along the top: Promise to whom?; Promise about…; Promise reminder is…. The chart will have 12 squares to fill in, and children should copy and complete the chart.

CLIPS

Explore the promises running through the Bible story.

On YouTube search "The Bible Project: Covenants" (5:45mins). Discuss the key ideas and list the 4 covenants. Or search "The Bible Project: Messiah" (5:47mins) and discuss the Bible story.

GO BIG TIMELINE

Make a giant timeline in order to lay out God's covenants and major Biblical events in order.

Equipment: *String, at least 10 sheets of A5 paper, felt-tip pens (and adhesive tack for a wall display)*

In groups of 4, children could create a timeline on the wall or on the floor. Children write out God's 4 covenants, any 5 major Biblical events, and 2 dates or times: Dawn of Time; 21st century. (More dates can be given: e.g. 2000 BC (Abraham), 1500 BC (Moses) ad 33 (Jesus).) These could be good ideas for events: the creation, the Fall, the flood, crossing the Red Sea, David and Goliath, the crucifixion. Offer plenty of help with dates and positioning. Children lay the string on the floor, with dates below and promises and events above it.

Sheet: Covenant Crossword

The answer page is at the back of the photocopiable sheets.

Sheet: Covenants Timeline

Make a timeline of God's promises.

Cut out events and promise markers and arrange them along the line. Place events above the line and promises below. Variation: children can add further events to the timeline, and even fulfilments if they already know them for Abrahamic and Davidic Covenants.

Sheet: Movie Poster

Tell a story through a promotional poster.

Choose a covenant and list the main details: title, characters, reminder. Then use the sheet to tell your covenant/story, adding a tag line, picture, reviews, and release date. Choose dates close to: Noahic – 2300 BC; Abrahamic – 2000 BC; Mosaic – 1500 BC; Davidic – 1000 BC.

FLEXI-TASK

ACT 3: COVENANTS
SCENE 2: THE ABRAHAMIC COVENANT

PRODUCTION NOTES

UNIT AIM

- *To see the direction for the Bible story*

UNIT CONTENT

- *The Abrahamic Covenant (in detail)*
- *God swears to keep his promises*

WIDE ANGLE: SETTING THE SCENE

Genesis 12 is the turning point of the Bible story. Before it, humans live apart from God without hope of friendship with him, scattered across the world. Genesis 12 shows that God will gather his own people to know and love him. God is reversing the effects of the Fall.

The Bible story is about how God fulfils the Abrahamic Covenant. God promises to give Abraham a land, and so Abraham goes to Canaan. The Bible story follows where Abraham's descendants live with God, and finishes in the new creation. God also promises Abraham a great nation – countless descendants like grains of sand on the seashore or stars in the sky. The New Testament shows how anyone with Abraham's faith is gathered into his nation, and they gather as a great crowd in the new creation. The crowd comes from all nations. And God promises Abraham blessing for any who bless him and curse for any who curse him. One of his descendants will bless the whole world.

Jesus fulfils the promises of the Abrahamic Covenant. In the new creation, he brings the great nation to live with him and he blesses them with forgiveness of sins. Genesis 12 points all the way to the new creation.

SCENE CARD

Stars: God promises Abraham his own land, countless descendants, and great blessing.

CLOSE-UP

The Abrahamic Covenant shows early signs of *God's Rescue*. The Tower of Babel builders want to be great, and God promises Abraham that he will "*make [his] name great*". God judges sin in Genesis 3–11, but here he promises to "*bless all nations on earth through you*". His nation will produce a Chosen One (Messiah) who will rule his people and rescue them from God's judgment.

FLASHBACK <<<

The blessing of Abraham echoes the blessing on humanity at creation. Both have a far-reaching purpose: humankind will rule and have children (1:28), and Abraham's descendants will be a blessing to the world (12:3).

FLASH-FORWARD >>>

God names his chosen people after Israel (Abraham's grandson, who is previously called Jacob), which means "he struggles with God". Israel will struggle between obeying and disobeying his authority. In the new creation, God makes a Jerusalem where none will reject him; multitudes of Abraham's descendants will worship him there (Revelation 7:9–10).

BONUS FEATURES ✪✪✪

Did you know?

- *Astronomers say there are more stars in the universe than grains of sand in the world's deserts and beaches. God promised Abraham as many children as the stars and sand. This countless number is said to be 25 figures long.*

ACTION PLANS

SCENE CARD

Stars: Consider how God promises Abraham countless children.

PRESENT STARS.

- *What did God promise Abraham?*
- *How many descendants will Abraham have (lead answers to "countless")?*
- *Why Abraham?*

Equipment: *Sand (or grains of salt)*

Hand out pinches of sand and estimate how many grains there are. Count the grains and consider how many children God promises Abraham! Scientists say there are more stars in the universe than grains of sand on the planet.

Word bank for 3-4 line summary:
promises, covenant, trust, land, children, nation, blessing.

ABRAHAM HOT SEATING

Interview Abraham on God's promises.

Choose a child to play Abraham. Invite open-ended questions from the students based on what they have learned. Everyone could practise using the key facts about Abraham and the promises God made to him. The child should answer factually and (where possible) emotionally. Abraham can wear a piece of clothing to help the drama, and rotate the child playing him.

Alternatively, children could write their questions down and read them out for some short discussions.

BINGO INFO

Play bingo with the facts on Abraham.

Children draw 9-square bingo grids and write down short, key bits of information in each square: e.g. phrases from the 3-part covenant, or Abraham's age. Read out possible answers; children cross out a box if they match their answers. They call "Bingo!" when they make a line of crossed out boxes (vertical, horizontal, or diagonal). Continue until someone has a full house (all squares are filled).

Alternatively, ask questions. If the children have written the answer, they can cross it out. When they call bingo, they say the answers they crossed out.

Sheet: Sorting Sentences 1

Sort God's 3 promises without talking.

Here's another way to use the Sorting Sentences sheet. In groups of 3–4, children cut out the 15 boxes and lay them face up on the table. Jumble them up and each take a roughly equal share. They should make 3 lines of 5 boxes to recreate the promises.

Rules: no talking and no taking. No demanding and no refusing. Children must look for who needs their spare phrases. Relax the rules if it's too challenging. Alternatively, the boxes could remain in the middle of the table and children take them one by one.

ACT 4: NATION ISRAEL
SCENE 1: GOD'S CAST FAMILY

PRODUCTION NOTES

UNIT AIM

- *To see how God builds Abraham's family*

UNIT CONTENT

- *Abraham travels to Canaan*
- *Abraham nearly sacrifices Isaac*
- *Isaac, Jacob, and Joseph's adventures*

WIDE ANGLE: SETTING THE SCENE

Abraham's family shows what it's like to trust God's promises. Abraham travels around 400–500 miles to Canaan; he trusts God for a son in his old age and Isaac is born when he is 100. Abraham obeys God so strongly that he is prepared to sacrifice his promised son for God. Isaac grows to trust God for a wife, and prays for a son too. He gets twins! Esau and Jacob fight, but they eventually trust God for their futures and the nation is named after Jacob, renamed "Israel". Israel means "he struggles with God". Israel too will struggle in their obedience and faith.

The Patriarchs (founding ancestral fathers of Israel) trust God for acceptance. They are far from perfect! Abraham lies to Pharaoh of Egypt. Isaac prefers Esau over Jacob, and Jacob cheats almost everyone he meets. But the promise never relied on them. God swears to Abraham that he will keep his promise on his own life (Genesis 15). God's Cast Family is a collection of people who trust God for acceptance, even though they sin. Abraham's faith is credited to him as righteousness. He isn't perfect, but his faith means God treats him as if he is guiltless before God. The same faith is shown by all of God's people in the Bible.

SCENE CARD

Family Tree: Abraham fathers his great nation, including Isaac, Jacob, and Joseph.

CLOSE-UP

The *Patriarchs'* names show how they trust God. Abraham, "father of many", remembers how God rewards his trust. Isaac, "he laughs", remembers how Sarah laughs at God's promise, and her joy at his birth. Jacob, "cheater", remembers how he treated his brother, father, and uncle, before he wrestles God and finally wants blessing. Jacob is renamed Israel, "he struggles with God", and Israel will struggle to trust God.

FLASH-FORWARD >>>

Mount Moriah was where Abraham almost sacrificed his son (Genesis 22:2), was where sacrifices were offered at Solomon's Temple (2 Chronicles 3:1), and was close to where God the Father sacrifices his Son, Jesus, at Golgotha (Matthew 27:33).

Jacob's 12 sons would form the names of Israel's 12 tribes after his death (49:28).

God surprisingly chose Jacob's cruellest son, Judah, for the family line of his chosen saviour (Matthew 1:2–3).

BONUS FEATURES ✪✪✪

Did you know?

- *Abraham's name is repeated 149 times, Isaac's name 55 times, and Jacob's name 178 times in the Bible after they die. Israel (or Israelites) is mentioned 2,431 times! These characters are hugely important.*

ACTION PLANS

SCENE CARD

Family Tree: Consider how God begins his nation with a family who trust him.

PRESENT FAMILY TREE.

- *Who are the oldest and youngest?*
- *Whose family are we studying and why?*
- *What shape will it be over thousands of years?*

Discuss how to draw family trees. Discuss how a tiny seed becomes a huge tree. Perhaps look at pictures of giant sequoias or mustard trees. Consider how all of God's people root back to Abraham.

Word bank for 3-4 line summary:
Patriarchs, descendants, nation, Israel, Abraham, Isaac, Jacob.

FAMILY TREE

Draw Abraham's family tree.

Show how to draw family trees – use equals signs for married couples, vertical lines for next generations, and horizontal lines to label children. Complete Abraham's family tree including these names: Abraham, Sarah, Isaac, Rebekah, Laban, Esau, Jacob, Jacob's sons, Joseph. Or look in the Bible to find extra names. Explore what each name means and write "Patriarch" next to the Patriarchs.

PATRIARCHS HOT SEATING

Interview the Patriarchs on how they trusted God.

After reading about each character, choose children to play Abraham, Isaac, Jacob, or Joseph, and any supporting characters. Invite open-ended questions from the students to hint at areas where the characters trusted God. The actors should enter into character and can wear a piece of clothing to help the drama. The characters showed trust in different ways: Abraham was quick to trust God, Isaac showed glimpses, but Jacob was very stubborn.

Alternatively, children could write their questions down and read them out for some short discussions.

Sheet: Mime Artists 1

Perform still poses for the scenes in the Patriarchs' lives.

Equipment: *Camera, casting sheets, tape*

Discuss how pictures tell a story. Children mime the scenes in the Patriarchs' lives for a set of photos. Use the Mime Artists sheets and cast the roles for the scenes. Children write their character's expression. Work in groups of 8–10 or altogether. Give 2 minutes to rehearse their poses for their performance. Position the camera and lay out tape to mark the edges of the stage. Encourage good body language to capture actions and emotions. Show the photos back to the students.

Alternatively, or afterward, try it as a speed exercise. Time the group(s), taking photos when each pose is ready. Review how the characters demonstrated their trust or lack of trust in God.

FLEXI-TASK

Sheet: Photo Album

Tell a long story with a few snapshots.

List parts of a person's life or a story, and use the sheet to illustrate it and title each scene. Choose a theme for the pictures, e.g. "How the Patriarchs trusted God", and add fun comments showing how they feel about their memories!

ACT 4: NATION ISRAEL
SCENE 2: GOD'S RESCUE

PRODUCTION NOTES

UNIT AIM

- *To see how God rescues his people*

UNIT CONTENT

- *God sends Moses back to Egypt*
- *The plagues, Passover, and exodus*

SCENE CARD

Rescue Ring: God uses Moses to rescue Israel from slavery, crossing the Red Sea to safety.

CLOSE-UP

God's Rescue involves payment. Israel sacrifices a perfect lamb in their place, showing each household that their sin deserves death and that another dies instead. They spread its blood on their doors to show their faith in this payment. God calls it a sign that they believe.

FLASH-FORWARD >>>

In the New Testament, John the Baptist saw Jesus and said, "Look, the Lamb of God, who takes away the sin of the world!" (John 1:29). The Passover story points to this "Passover Lamb" who also died at Passover time (1 Corinthians 5:7), to deal with a much greater problem than slavery.

BONUS FEATURES ✪✪✪

Did you know?

- *Jewish families still read and perform the Passover story every year. The youngest child begins the celebration by asking, "Why is this night different from all other nights?" They relive the story as they eat the Seder plate with its symbolic foods - including a shank bone, bitter herbs, and nut mixture.*

- *During the last plague God saves the firstborn sons of Israel, and God calls Israel his firstborn son (Exodus 4:22) and then saves all of Israel. Passover is a microcosm for the exodus.*

WIDE ANGLE: SETTING THE SCENE

400 years later, God reveals himself as a rescuer. Israel has been living in Egypt since the time of Joseph, but they are now Pharaoh's slaves, who orders that all Hebrew sons be drowned in the River Nile. Egypt is incredibly rich and powerful, and there's no escape for the Hebrews. All God's people can do is pray for rescue. Away on Mount Sinai, Moses has been a refugee from Egypt for 40 years. Having grown up as an Egyptian prince, he had discovered that he was a Hebrew and killed an Egyptian slave driver. He feels unable to rescue God's people himself. God comes to him at the burning bush and calls himself "I AM" – he is above all gods and will show his power to Pharaoh.

The Passover and exodus show how God rescues. After a series of plagues wipe out Egypt's wealth and economy, Moses tells Pharaoh that all firstborn sons in Egypt will die. This includes the Hebrew boys. But God makes a way out – a rescue plan. The Hebrews must sacrifice a lamb and spread its blood on their doors as a sign that they trust its blood to pay for their firstborns: Life for life and blood for blood. The New Testament tells how Jesus is a Passover Lamb who dies for his people: life for life and blood for blood. His people only need to trust his blood for their rescue. And any can be rescued – note how a mixed crowd leave Egypt with God's people. God rescues through sacrifice and faith.

ACTION PLANS

SCENE CARD

Rescue Ring: Consider how God rescues his people from slavery.

PRESENT RESCUE RING.

- *Who needs these?*
- *Why might God's people need this?*

Discuss how God's people were trapped in Egypt as slaves and prayed for a rescue. See what the children know about the rescue. Compare a water rescue with God's rescue – who's bringing the rescue, and how many are rescued?

Word bank for 3–4 line summary:
Pharaoh, Moses, burning bush, plagues, Passover, exodus.

CHARACTER REVERSALS

Discuss character arcs and how they make great stories.

Which characters change in famous stories? Consider some who change from bad to good, or vice versa. Offer these as ideas: *Star Wars* (Darth Vader); *Finding Nemo* (Marlin, Nemo's dad); *Harry Potter* (Severus Snape); *Robin Hood* (Friar Tuck). Link this to Moses. How did he change? Note that Moses killed the slave driver when he was 40 years old, and met God when he was 80. He led the Hebrews as an old man for 40 years, and died aged 120.

CLIP

Explore God's name - Lord or Yahweh.

On YouTube search "The Bible Project: Word Study: YHWH – 'LORD'" (3:59mins). Discuss the key ideas and how God identified himself to Moses.

RESEARCH THE PLAGUES

Look up how each plague damaged Egypt.

List the 10 plagues. Write explanations for how each plague would have damaged Egypt's economy and way of life: e.g. Plague 1: the Nile turns to blood – the fish die, the river stinks, and the Egyptians cannot drink. Try ranking the plagues according to: damage done, biggest sign of God, annoyance factor!

Sheet: Journey Mapping

Plot Israel's journeys to and from Egypt.

Complete the sheet and plot these movements on the map. (Leave space for further journeys: Mount Sinai to Canaan, and wandering in the Desert.)

1. Canaan to Egypt: *Joseph goes to Egypt as a slave. His family later moves there*
2. Egypt to Midian: *Moses escapes to Midian after killing an Egyptian slave driver*
3. Midian to Egypt: *Moses meets God at the burning bush and he returns to Pharaoh*
4. Egypt to Midian: *Israel crosses the Red Sea and arrives at Mount Sinai*

ACTING MOSES' LIFE

Perform Moses' life in 4 stages.

Create 4 groups to each act out one of these scenes from *The Blockbuster Bible*: Moses' birth, the burning bush, the plagues and Passover, the exodus. Cast Moses in each group and choose a prop for Moses to carry. As teacher, play the director and make the scenes run from one into the next. Film the activity if there's time to watch it back.

Sheet: Newspaper Front Page

Write a newspaper story reporting on God's Rescue in Egypt.

Sheet: Exodus Snakes and Ladders

Test each other on knowledge of the exodus.

Discuss how difficult the slaves found getting their freedom. Write a list of episodes on the board: Moses' birth, the burning bush, the plagues, Passover, exodus.

Play Snakes and Ladders in groups of 3–4. When children reach a snake or a ladder, they must ask each other a question on the unit to avoid going down or to earn going up. Keep questions possible, and interesting! Use erasers, etc. as playing pieces, and use a spinner or dice.

ACT 4: NATION ISRAEL
SCENE 3: GOD'S SPECIAL EFFECTS

PRODUCTION NOTES

UNIT AIM

- *To see how God blesses Israel*

UNIT CONTENT

- *God gives the Law*
- *God gives himself, living in the tabernacle*
- *God gives a system of sacrifices*

WIDE ANGLE: SETTING THE SCENE

God continues to fulfil his promises to Abraham. After rescuing his people, he means to bless them. Having banished them from Eden, he gathers them at Mount Sinai for 3 big gifts. He marks the occasion with thunder, fire, and trumpet sounds over the mountain. God's blessings have very special effects.

God makes a new covenant, the Mosaic Covenant. He tells Israel that he will treasure them if they obey him fully and keep his laws and covenant. His already-rescued people must now obey him. They don't obey him to be rescued; they obey him in response to the past. The Law, stored in the ark of the covenant, shows them how. It's a return to the days of Eden – God's people can obey him and enjoy his blessings.

The tabernacle is another return to Eden. God tells them to build a portable tent for him in the desert – a "tent of meeting". It's decorated with images of Eden: the cherubim guarding the east side, and the tree-like symbols inside. Israel is living with God. In Revelation, the new creation also has images of Eden: the tree of life and a crystal-clear river. God rescues his people to live with them.

The sacrificial system makes living with God possible. On the Day of Atonement, the high priest takes 2 goats and makes payment for their people's sin. One goat dies, and the other is banished into the desert to carry their blame away. They can stand clean before him.

SCENE CARD

Three Gifts: God gives Israel 3 blessings – Law, tabernacle to live with them, and sacrifices.

CLOSE-UP

The tabernacle reminds Israel about *Living with God*. But it reminds Israel that God is holy and they must be clean (forgiven). Its thick dividing curtain cuts the sinful people off from their God. Only the high priest enters on one day per year. The tabernacle allows God's people to live with him and not die.

FLASHBACK <<<

The tabernacle is like Eden. Both are attended by cherubim and are entered from the east. The lampstand could represent the tree of life, and the stones in Eden are in the tabernacle.

FLASH-FORWARD >>>

In the New Testament John says Jesus is God "tabernacling" with his people. He says "the Word became flesh and made his dwelling" (or "pitched his tent") among his people (John 1:14). John says God tabernacles with his people in person.

The Temple curtain separated the sinful people from their holy God. When Jesus dies, the barrier is torn down. They can live with God again.

BONUS FEATURES ✪✪✪

Did you know?

- *In the movie* Raiders of the Lost Ark, *Indiana Jones says an army that carries the ark is invincible. It brought blessing to Israel and curse to its enemies when it was captured (1 Samuel 5:10–12). Today, no one knows where it is.*

- *There were not just 10 commandments; there were 613. These 10 were foundational to all the rest, which unpack the details.*

- *Moses smashed the stone tablets (Exodus 32), and had to rewrite them himself (34:28). When he came down the mountain, his face was shining so brightly he had to veil it.*

ACTION PLANS

SCENE CARD

Three Gifts: Consider how God blesses his people with gifts in the desert.

PRESENT THREE GIFTS.

- *Why do we give gifts?*
- *Whose birthday is God celebrating?*
- *What effect should gifts have?*

Discuss how God celebrated Israel's birthday – the nation is born! Discuss how God wants his people to have different gifts to any other nation, to help them to be different and to love him. Consider how someone's presence is sometimes the best present.

Word bank for 3-4 line summary:
blessings, gifts, Law, tabernacle, live, sacrifices, blood.

RULES AND RULERS

Play a game to show how rules are best when they're given to us.

Create groups of 6 and nominate leaders. Aim of the game: find as many purposes for a ruler as you can in 3 minutes, but the group leaders must set the rules! Quietly choose a special group and give them these rules:

- *"No one can get hurt"*
- *"Be hygienic - it shouldn't go in the mouth"*
- *"Do not break the ruler."*

Review the leaders' rules. Discuss the rules given to the special group and why they were given. Link to how God gave the Ten Commandments to support life and goodness and make one nation special.

THUMBOMETER

Measure opinions on the Ten Commandments.
Gather knowledge or views on the Ten Commandments using a voting system – thumbs up, thumbs down, and wavering thumbs. True or false knowledge. List the Ten Commandments but slip in fakes like recycling, swearing, and greed.

Opinion polls – if they could have only 10 laws, which would they have? Include silly things like limiting sweet-eating/banning Brussel sprouts. What are laws for?

CLIPS

Explore Law, sacrifice, and atonement.

On YouTube search *The Bible Project: The Law* (5:59mins). Discuss the key ideas. Also try *The Bible Project: Sacrifice and Atonement in the Bible* (6:10mins) and discuss the key ideas.

BLIND DRAWING

Draw the tabernacle following someone's describing skills.

In pairs or as a group, show the tabernacle to one child. They will describe how to draw it to another, who cannot see the drawing(s). Pairs can sit back to back but avoid prying eyes. Give 5 minutes. Compare the result with the real thing.

Sheet: Tablet for Living

Explain the reasons for the Law, tabernacle, and the sacrifices.

Sheet: Designs for Israel

Complete 4 gift cards with descriptions for God's gifts.

Sheet: Build a Tabernacle

Speed-build a tabernacle.

Equipment: *Play dough, modelling clay, or plasticine.*
Building activity: Make groups of 3-4. Hand them the tabernacle templates and play dough (or use stationery). In 5–7 minutes, the children build the tabernacle on the paper. Follow the wall outlines and make the objects. Which will be the best? It took the Israelites about half a year!

Memory game: as above, but without the templates. Groups learn the parts of the tabernacle and label their models with slips of paper. Or try moving the groups around to finish others' models, or children take turns to check the picture on the teacher's desk.

Review the creations and hand a Michelangelo Sculpture Prize to the winning group. Discuss who is missing from the creation: the cloud of God's presence. Why does God want to live in the middle of the Israelite camp?

ACT 4: NATION ISRAEL
SCENE 4: GOD'S LOCATION SCOUT

PRODUCTION NOTES

UNIT AIM

- *To see how God leads Israel to its land*

UNIT CONTENT

- *The scouting mission into Canaan*
- *The bronze snake*
- *Blessings and curses for Israel*

WIDE ANGLE: SETTING THE SCENE

Israel slips up in its first steps. They have seen 10 plagues, the Red Sea parted, and the thunder, fire, and trumpet sounds over Sinai, but they fail to trust God. They show why they are called Israel – they "struggle with God". In the Abrahamic Covenant, God promises Israel their own land, and the 12 location scouts entering Canaan find great reasons to enter. The land is so fruitful! They tell the waiting Israelites how it flows with milk and honey, and show them its figs and pomegranates. But old habits die hard. They report on the giants living in strong cities, and beg to return to Egypt. They haven't learned to trust God.

God trains his people to trust him. He sends them to wander in the desert for 40 years; none from this generation will enter the Promised Land except Joshua and Caleb, the 2 spies who trust him. In this time they complain about the food he gives them (manna and quail), so God sends venomous snakes among them. Anyone bitten dies. They cry out for rescue again, and God tells Moses to put a bronze snake on a pole. Anyone bitten may look at it and live. This training will be useful when they enter the land, but the same training applies to all God's people. When they look at and trust Jesus on the cross, God also rescues them from their sin. God's blessings only come to those who trust him.

SCENE CARD

Milk and Honey: Moses sends 12 spies into Canaan, but Israel fears the giants there and rebels.

CLOSE-UP

The 10 spies exaggerate to dismay their hearers. "The land we explored devours those living in it. All the people we saw there are of great size. We saw the Nephilim there (the descendants of Anak come from the Nephilim). We seemed like grasshoppers in our own eyes, and we looked the same to them" (Numbers 13:32–33). The Nephilim were giants living before Noah's flood, so mentioning them is likely an excuse rather than true.

FLASH-FORWARD >>>

God fulfilled his promise to scatter his people if they disobeyed him. In 722 BC Assyria decimated Israel, and Babylon took captives away from Judah in 605 BC, and in 586 BC when they destroyed Jerusalem.

BONUS FEATURES ✪✪✪

Did you know?

- *The Canaanites were giants. The tallest people today measure over 2.4 metres (8 feet), due to a rare condition called gigantism.*

- *Israel has a perfect climate for growing fruit. Whereas only 6 different fruits are mentioned in the Bible, over 40 are grown in the area today.*

ACTION PLANS

SCENE CARD

Milk and Honey: Consider how God's people react when they see their land.

PRESENT MILK AND HONEY.

- *What kind of land produces milk and honey?*
- *Why could God's people trust him when they entered the land?*

Discuss how God chose Israel, rescued them, and blessed them. Discuss the type of land God will give them and the kind of life they will have there.

Word bank for 3–4 line summary:
spies, explore, Joshua, Caleb, giants, fruit, wander.

BINGO MEANINGS

Play bingo to think about the events of the journey.

Children draw a 9-square bingo grid (3x3). Make sure it's big enough for short phrases. Write 9 important phrases or words from the chapter, e.g. 12 spies, milk and honey, wandering for 40 years. Read out clue phrases, and children cross words off when they recognize their answers; e.g. after saying "12 who entered the land" they can cross off "12 spies". They call "Bingo!" when they have a line (horizontal, vertical, or diagonal), and then a full house when all squares are filled.

   Avoid reading through the children's answers before giving the questions. Decide whether one-word answers count.

VERBAL TENNIS

Play a quick-fire word association game, testing who knows the keywords best.

Invite children to memorize the keywords in this chapter, ready for a game of Verbal Tennis. Children sit in pairs opposite each other and say a keyword back and forth at each other. Scoring like tennis: 15–love, 30–love, 30–15, 40–15, game. Rules: no repeats in the same point, no hesitating, umming, erring, or deviating.

E.g. (1) "Moses!" (2) "Giants!" (1) "Desert!" (2) "Sinai!" (1) "Milk!" (2) "Umm!" (1) "Point to me! 15–love."

Play best of 3 games. To extend the activity, children could avoid using the same words in consecutive games.

MIME ACTING

Perform the scouting mission without talking.

Capture the feelings of the characters in the story through mime. Show the characters' excitement, shock, despair, determination, and depression. Allocate the roles: Moses, 10 spies, Joshua, Caleb, Israelites, voice of God. As teacher, play the director and gesture to the actors to interject when it's their time. Film the activity if there's time to watch it back.

Sheet: Scouting Mission Feelings Graph

Plot a graph showing how the location scouting mission into the Promised Land went.

ACT 4: NATION ISRAEL
SCENE 5: GOD'S STAGE

PRODUCTION NOTES

UNIT AIM

- *To see how God hands Canaan over to Israel*

UNIT CONTENT

- *Rahab and the spies*
- *Crossing the River Jordan*
- *Circling Jericho*

WIDE ANGLE: SETTING THE SCENE

God's training in faith pays off. He brings the Israelites to the Promised Land and they must do some odd things to take the land. When they arrive at the River Jordan, Joshua gives everyone their roles. The priests carrying the ark of the covenant (containing the Ten Commandments) walk into the river first and stand in it until everyone has crossed! Miraculously, the river stops flowing and the Israelites cross easily. Once in Canaan, Israel is called a nation and they must continue to trust God. Their circling of Jericho for 7 days, before watching its huge walls fall down, also comes from their training in faith. God's people are obeying him and enjoying his blessings.

God and Israel must act together. Even though God can reduce the cities to rubble, Israel must obey him. One will not happen without the other. The training in faith should lead to obedience. God has already rescued his people and they must make every effort to respond carefully. They must take the whole land. In Joshua 10, God even stops the sun in the sky so they can finish a battle in daylight. But taking the land involves exiling or killing its inhabitants, who worship other gods and often sacrifice their children to them. In the end, they fail to finish the job. God fulfils his promises to Abraham (land, children, blessing), but he will not reward their disobedience…

SCENE CARD

Rubble: The next generation conquer Canaan and God turns Jericho to rubble.

CLOSE-UP

The Canaan Conquest teaches Israel faith. At the Jordan, God tells the priests carrying the ark to stand in the river while everyone passes by. Usually, the river would be 3m deep and 30m wide. As soon as they stepped out, the river's flow began again. At Jericho, Joshua calls his people to shout as a sign of their faith (6:5). The shout didn't make the walls fall down, but shows they expect them to.

FLASH-FORWARD >>>

A later king rebuilds Jericho, despite Joshua's curse against doing so. King Hiel of Bethel suffers for it. His firstborn and youngest sons die (1 Kings 16:34).

BONUS FEATURES ✪✪✪

Did you know?

- *When Israel entered the Promised Land, they began to be referred to as a nation (Joshua 3:17). When they lived in Egypt and the desert, they were only a people.*

ACTION PLANS

SCENE CARD

Rubble: Consider how God wins the land for Israel.

PRESENT RUBBLE.

- *Where does rubble come from?*
- *What scared Israel about the land?*
- *Who will conquer the land – God or Israel?*

Discuss how God wants to conquer the land alongside his people: both together. Discuss how God wants to build his people's trust.

Word bank for 3-4 line summary:
Jordan, Jericho, nation, trust, destroy, fight, land.

SPOT THE MISTAKE

Challenge the children's memory by retelling the stories with mistakes.

Hand out slips of paper – one red and the other green. Otherwise, the children can quickly colour the slips in. Retell the stories with mistakes – the children hold up the green when they think the details are true, and red for false.

Embellish the story with exaggerated details, character inaccuracies, and detail changes. Range from the subtle to the ridiculous.

MOOD MUSIC

Stir the senses for reading the Canaan Conquest.

Play some music while reading the River Jordan Crossing and Circling of Jericho. Perhaps use an action/adventure movie soundtrack like *The Lord of the Rings* or tracks like *Ride of the Valkyries* by Wagner. Read through the stage directions with the most bellowing and dramatic voices possible.

Alternatively, save the Mood Music for acting to. Fade the music out when the drama closes.

DIVIDING THE LAND

Research how the 12 tribes got their land.

Look up Jacob's 12 sons' names in Genesis 35:23–26. Then look up a map of the 12 tribes of Israel. Which two aren't from Jacob's sons? Explain that Joseph's two sons (Ephraim and Manasseh) had land as half-tribes, and the Levites worked as priests across Israel.

FURNITURE ACTING

Perform the Canaan Conquest using tables and chairs as much as possible.

Equipment: *Camera, casting sheets, tape*

List and cast the characters: Joshua, the priests, God, the soldiers, the 12, the people. Read or recap the Canaan Conquest, drawing children's attention to their parts. Give 2 minutes to read over their roles. What could the furniture be used to make? (Perhaps a table with chairs on could be the Ark of the Covenant.) Set up the River Jordan and city of Jericho using the furniture, ensuring there's space to part the "river" and circle the "city" easily and safely.

Perhaps hand out props like rams' horns and swords. Film the activity if there's time to watch it back.

Sheet: Conquest Cast List

Write a theatre programme for the Canaan Conquest.

Sheet: Scriptwriting

Write a script and stage directions.

FLEXI-TASK

Explain how scriptwriters tell a story through speech. Some lines will be long and others short. Sometimes people interrupt. Sometimes people get angry, or excited, or tired.

Turn the play scripts in the book into one script. Joshua can be the only one speaking, or it can include multiple speakers. Who will win the Best Adapted Screenplay Award? Start the script together on the whiteboard for the first line or 2, avoiding writing lines more than 2 lines long.

ACT 4: NATION ISRAEL
SCENE 6: GOD'S JUDGES

PRODUCTION NOTES

UNIT AIM

- *To see how God brings Judges to save Israel*

UNIT CONTENT

- *Ehud defeats the Moabites*
- *Deborah defeats the Canaanites*
- *Gideon defeats the Midianites*
- *Samson defeats the Philistines*

WIDE ANGLE: SETTING THE SCENE

Israel's disobedience leads to a cycle of sin and rescue. They fail to exile or kill their immoral neighbours as instructed, and begin to marry Canaanite women. Moses warned against this in Deuteronomy: if anyone intermarries with the foreigners, their hearts will turn from God; Israel forgets who they are. They are God's rescued people, but they worship foreign gods. They break the Mosaic Covenant, but God is committed to their obedience. He brings foreign armies to rule over them until they will pray for rescue. This happens again and again for 200–300 years: Israel worships foreign gods, God brings a foreign army to rule them, they pray, God brings a Judge, the Judge defeats the enemy, Israel enjoys peace, and then returns to the foreign gods.

The Judges are good rescuers, but not good examples. A refrain appears 4 times in the book of Judges: "In those days Israel had no king", and twice adds: "Everyone did as they saw fit." Israel needs a leader who will help them obey God. The Judges defeat the foreign armies, but they don't always set the best examples of godly (god-like) living. Even though Ehud, Deborah, and Gideon show faith in desperate times, disobedient Samson is equally used by God. Samson breaks 3 of the commandments, but God still blesses him with his Spirit's power. In the New Testament, God gives all believers the Spirit's power to obey him, and they have a godly king to copy. Israel needs a good and godly leader.

SCENE CARD

Downward Trend Graph: Foreign kings conquer rebellious Israel, who pray for rescuing leaders: Judges.

CLOSE-UP

God's Rescue is helped by God's Spirit. God chooses unlikely men (and women), and his Spirit often comes upon them powerfully to defeat their enemies. Gideon calls men to arms to fight the Midianites. Samson can tear a lion apart with his hands, and kill 1,000 Philistines with a donkey's jawbone.

FLASH-FORWARD >>>

God's Spirit empowers future leaders too. The Spirit comes powerfully on Saul at his coronation and upon David as he was chosen to be the next king. In the New Testament, God's Spirit anoints Jesus as the Chosen One (Messiah) and promised king. God's Spirit also strengthens all Jesus' followers from Pentecost onwards.

BONUS FEATURES ✪✪✪

Did you know?

- *There are 12 judges mentioned in the book of Judges, and the Hebrew word shofetim may be translated as "leaders" or "chieftains". They exist ultimately as a warning not to treat their relationship with God carelessly.*
- *The book of Ruth happens during the time of Judges.*

ACTION PLANS

SCENE CARD

Downward Trend Graph: Consider how Israel needs faithful leaders.

PRESENT DOWNWARD TREND GRAPH.

- *How do leaders help Israel?*
- *What happens after Joshua dies?*
- *What are the ups and downs on the graph?*

Discuss how Israel obeys and disobeys God for 200–300 years. Discuss how God sends enemies to make his people trust him, and then rescues them with Judges (leaders).

Word bank for 3-4 line summary:
Joshua, idols, enemies, pray, Judges, Samson, 200-300.

NEED FOR LEADERS

Play "spot the leader" without a leader.

Children sit or stand in a circle. One child (the "spotter") stands in the middle with eyes closed. Silently nominate a leader and everyone copies their actions. The "spotter" must spot the leader. Repeat the game, always changing the spotter and beginning with the same action. After a few rounds, don't nominate a leader. Everyone begins with the same action again. The spotter looks for a leader but everyone will inevitably "do as they see fit".

Review the exercise. How did people feel in each game? What happened in the last round? Why? Link to Israel lacking leadership for 200–300 years! The Judges led for short periods but the people wanted kings.

JUDGES HOT SEATING

Interview the Judges on how they led Israel.

Read the Judges' acceptance speeches and choose children to play Gideon and Samson. Interview them at the same time or separately. Invite open-ended questions from the students to consider how they led Israel. Compare the two Judges: personality; power; popularity; prayers. The actors dress or carry things to suggest weakness or "thugness".

Alternatively, children could write their questions down and read them out for some short discussions.

PERFORMANCE MONOLOGUES

Perform the Judges' acceptance speeches without notes.

Equipment: *Podium (table on its end) and microphone, ruler, or board pen*

Read an acceptance speech and recap the challenges the Judges faced and how they led or saved Israel. Set up a podium at the front of the room. Invite a pupil to give a Judge's acceptance speech behind the podium, holding the microphone. Review the personality and points. Repeat performing until it serves its purpose, or move onto a new Judge.

FLEXI-TASK

Sheet: Movie Certificate

Explain why the Judges' lives are 18-rated.

Hand out the movie certificate and discuss age ratings. Write a guide to the violent content in the Judges' lives. Use phrases like: *"There is a scene where…"* or *"There is a brief…"* *"The movie includes…"* See the BBFC/MPAA ratings guides for examples. Begin the certificate on the board: e.g. *"In one scene, Ehud pulls out his sword and thrusts it into Eglon's fat belly."*

Or complete the sheet on one Judge. Describe all the things that might be bad, or explain why violence happens in this Judge's story.

Sheet: Acceptance Speech (Best Judge)

Choose a Judge and write a speech explaining how they led Israel.

ACT 4: NATION ISRAEL
SCENE 7: GOD'S KINGS

PRODUCTION NOTES

UNIT AIM

- *To see how 3 kings lead God's nation*

UNIT CONTENT

- *Saul rules for himself*
- *David rules for God*
- *Solomon's highs and lows*
- *The Divided Kingdom*

SCENE CARD

Crown: Israel wants kings like other nations, and God promises David an eternal kingdom.

CLOSE-UP

The Davidic Covenant combines the themes of *God's Promises* and *God's Rescue*. God promises David a ruling dynasty: "Your house and your kingdom will last forever before me" (2 Samuel 7:16). God promises to rescue his people and lead them to obey him. The Messiah is this Chosen One.

FLASH-FORWARD >>>

Blind Bartimaeus calls Jesus the Son of David. Matthew calls Jesus the Messiah, the Son of David (Matthew 1:1). Jesus calls himself the Root and Offspring of David in John's revelation of heaven (Revelation 22:16).

BONUS FEATURES ✪✪✪

Did you know?

- *David had many skills. He was a musician who played the lyre in Saul's courts. He was a poet and songwriter who wrote around 75 Psalms. And he was a hugely successful general who led armies and even directed the invasion of Jerusalem through a water shaft when it was a Jebusite stronghold. The archaeologist Sir Charles Warren found such a shaft and tunnel (now Warren's Shaft) in 1867 and tourists can now climb it.*

WIDE ANGLE: SETTING THE SCENE

Israel needs a godly leader. They cry out for a king, but with bad motives. They want a king to rule instead of God, not to rule them under God. They want a rescuer king more than their rescuer God. Instead, they need a leader who loves God and leads his people to obey him.

Saul is a bad start for Israel. He looks great! He's tall, strong, and handsome. But his heart isn't committed to God's ways, and soon he disobeys God's instructions. Israel doesn't have its perfect leader. He makes excuses for his sin and God promises to tear his kingdom away from him.

David is a bright light. God chooses the young shepherd boy because David has a heart for God, and will lead his people to do the same. When he sins (he commits adultery with Bathsheba and murders her husband!), he doesn't make excuses like Saul. He seeks God's forgiveness.

Solomon starts well. He wants wisdom to lead, but his life turns to excess. He spends 7 years building God's Temple so that God lives with his people, but 13 years building his own palace. He taxes his people harshly and even marries 700 women, many of them foreign. His heart turns from God, who divides his kingdom in two.

In the Davidic Covenant, God promises the perfect king. God will establish David's throne forever and one of his descendants will rule God's people for eternity. Now Israel waits for a "Son of David".

ACTION PLANS

SCENE CARD

Crown: Consider how God leads his people through kings.

PRESENT CROWN.

- *What are kings and queens for?*
- *Who do they serve - us or God?*
- *Why did Israel need a king?*

Discuss Israel's need for a king and a family line. Discuss how a king needs to lead like Moses or Joshua, to lead Israel to trust God.

Word bank for 3-4 line summary:
Saul, excuses, David, faithful, eternal king, Solomon, idols.

KING/QUEEN CHILD

Hand supreme authority to one child and see who they rule for.

Choose a child to be king or queen. The teacher is their willing enforcement agency. The ruler must set up a kingdom with living quarters and others must obey. Or they give another task that reflects who the king serves first. The ruler's instructions should reveal whether they served themselves or their people. If appropriate, they can send others out (leaving the door open so they can watch).

Review who they ruled for/served. Link to Israel's kings. Who will they serve? Who should they rule for – themselves, others, or God? What makes a godly, God-loving king?

GUESS WHO: ISRAEL'S LEADERS

Play "Guess Who" to recap Israel's leaders.

List Israel's leaders since God first spoke to Abraham. Children choose a name and write it on a slip of paper or a playing card or use the sheet on page 118 if preferred. They must identify the person with the fewest questions possible. Either play as a group (one child stands in front) or play in pairs. Leaders include Abraham, Isaac, Jacob, Joseph, Moses, Joshua, Caleb, Gideon, Samson, Saul, David, Solomon.

Alternatively, play the party game version. Write the names on sheets/cards, shuffle them, and hand them out to stick on their foreheads. Children identify themselves with the fewest questions.

INTERVIEW READING

Read and perform the interviews.

Read through the interviews, with the teacher playing the interviewer and children playing each king. Dramatize the questioning to encourage dramatic answering. Perhaps use a prop to denote who is the king (a pencil case crown or ruler sceptre). Two children could stand at the front and silently mime what the king says. Afterward, ask the interviewer's questions to individuals and challenge them to answer in the king's way.

Review the kings' personalities and their successes and failings as kings.

KINGS HOT SEATING

Interview the kings on how they led Israel.

Equipment: *Crowns and sceptres – or empty pencil cases and rulers!*

Recap the differences between David and Solomon: whom they served first; their successes; their failings. Invite two children to play the kings. David should be humble and want God's glory most of all. Solomon should be over-the-top and show that he wants to glorify himself through his wealth and wives. Reward interviewers for good questions, and reward the kings for their knowledge and delivery. The actors wear crowns and hold sceptres.

Sheet: Questioning the Kings

Use The Blockbuster Bible to complete conversations with David and Solomon.

Sheet: Judges and Kings Crossword

The answer page is at the back of the photocopiable sheets.

Sheet: Playing Cards

Complete playing cards on any of the kings, scoring them on six categories.

You can complete this activity on many characters and form a pack of playing cards. The teacher should moderate the scores on each card.

FLEXI-TASK

ACT 5: PROPHETS AND KINGS
SCENE 1: WARNING AND HOPE!

PRODUCTION NOTES

UNIT AIM

- *To see how prophets guide God's people*

UNIT CONTENT

- *Messages of warning and hope to Israel*
- *Messages of warning and hope to Judah*
- *Daniel teaches Babylon's kings*
- *Ezra and Nehemiah reform Israel*
- *Esther helps rescue the Jews across Persia*
- *Jonah speaks to Nineveh*

WIDE ANGLE: SETTING THE SCENE

Israel forgets the Mosaic Covenant and their problem spirals. Moses warned the people before he died: obey God, and enjoy his blessings; disobey, and suffer his curses. God will scatter them if they break his covenant.

The prophets bring the same warnings. God divides the kingdom in two: Israel in the north and Judah in the south (with Jerusalem as its capital). Both kingdoms hear God's warnings against turning to other gods. In the northern kingdom, Elijah warns King Ahab against worshipping Baal until, after many warnings, God brings the Assyrian army in 722 BC to decimate Israel. The northern kingdom is finished.

In the south, prophets bring the same warnings to Judah. Isaiah, Jeremiah, and Ezekiel warn against the people's sin, but Judah largely rejects God's messengers. In 586 BC, God brings the Babylonian army to destroy Jerusalem and take its people into exile. God's people no longer live with God.

There's still hope for the exiles. God promised through Isaiah that a remnant will return. Ezekiel sees a vision: a valley of dry bones comes to life and forms a vast army. God's people will return to Jerusalem and he will give them a new heart that loves to obey him. In the New Testament, the Spirit comes at Pentecost to provide just this.

SCENE CARD

Signpost: Prophets warn Israel to turn back to God, and promise hope of return after exile.

CLOSE-UP

God's Rescue in the future is getting clearer. It will involve a new covenant. Ezekiel sees a valley full of very dry bones and God puts breath into them. The word for "breath" also means "Spirit". He will agree to give them life by his Spirit, and change their heart of stone for a heart of flesh that wants to obey him.

FLASHBACK <<<

The valley of dry bones reminds how God breathes life into Adam and Eve in the Garden of Eden.

FLASH-FORWARD >>>

The Spirit comes at Pentecost to help his people obey him. Before this, the Spirit only comes to certain people at certain times (Gideon, Samson, Saul, David).

BONUS FEATURES ✪✪✪
Did you know?

- *The empire of Assyria was replaced by the Babylonian empire, which was replaced by the Persian empire. They were the greatest empires in the ancient world. Persia even extended from Ethiopia to India!*

- *The prophets have interesting names. Elijah means "my God is Yahweh". Isaiah means "Yahweh is salvation". Jeremiah means "Yahweh will lift up". Ezekiel means "God strengthens". Daniel means "God is my judge". Jonah means "dove".*

- *Isaiah is quoted over 20 times in the New Testament in reference to Jesus as the promised Messiah.*

ACTION PLANS

SCENE CARD

Signpost: Consider how God gives his people two messages.

PRESENT SIGNPOST.

- *Why might people ignore signposts?*
- *Why might the prophets make good signposts?*

Recall how the kings often led for themselves and abandoned God. Discuss how God sent messengers (prophets) to guide the kings and his people back to him. Discuss the two main signs: warning and hope.

Word bank for 3–4 line summary:
prophets, warning, hope, obey, exile, return (Elijah/Isaiah/Jeremiah/Ezekiel).

FOLLOWING SIGNPOSTS

Consider how signposts demand a response.

Test obedience and understanding of signposts by presenting a series of road signs for the students to obey. Run back and forth through 10 road signs; intersperse 3–4 different stop signs. Discuss testing understanding and obedience, and why the kings need signposts. Who does the message come from?

DON'T SHOOT THE MESSENGER

Consider how messengers invite frustration.

Play an "obey the messenger" game. One child passes on the teacher's messages for the students to mime or obey. Leave the door open before starting! Ideas: work really hard; open exercise books; do 5 press-ups; salute their neighbour; do 10 star jumps; pretend to play a sport; stop playing football/rugby/tennis; leave the room if you didn't stop; tuck your shirts in; bow down before the teacher.

Review the exercise. Why did some not obey? How do you feel about the messenger? Link to Israel rejecting God's prophets.

Sheet: Prophets Crossword

The answer page is at the back of the photocopiable sheets.

Sheet: Speedy Prophets Timeline

Line up a timeline of events as quickly as possible.

Cut out and arrange the dates and events in order. Repeat the exercise to improve it and test understanding. This is most fun when it's a competition in speed. Choose an approach…

- Cardholders and directors. Cardholders line up along a wall and the rest of the students direct them (cardholders hold 2 if they need to). Children with date cards kneel in front of relevant events. Cardholders cannot look at other cards. Time them and swap roles to see who the quicker directors are.
- ¾ circle. Cardholders stand in a ¾ circle so they can see each other's cards. In silence they line up in order. Children with date cards kneel in front of relevant events. All children can see each other's other cards. Time them, swap, and repeat.
- Small groups. Children arrange the cards on a desk with dates and names above the events and speech.
- Individual work. Children arrange the cards in their books. They draw arrows to denote the passage of time.

POSTCARDS FROM FAR AWAY

Write and send postcards with the prophets' messages.

Equipment: *Postcards or card*

Recap the prophets' messages of warning and hope. Write the postcards and sign off as the prophet; send them to each other. Perhaps draw a destroyed Jerusalem or a picture of the prophecy on the reverse.

Sheets: Social Media

Tell messages through modern mediums.

Use the sheets to report a story or spread a message: CityChat, Snapscroll, eMessenger, Livestream. Follow the examples across "Warning and Hope!"

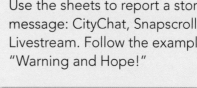

FLEXI-TASK

ACT 5: PROPHETS AND KINGS
SCENE 2: GLIMPSES OF THE MESSIAH

PRODUCTION NOTES

UNIT AIM

- *To see what the Messiah will do*

UNIT CONTENT

- *The Messiah's main roles*
- *The Messiah's birth*
- *The Messiah's death*

WIDE ANGLE: SETTING THE SCENE

The Old Testament story builds up to this. Humans have fallen from their perfect state and are trapped in their "sinful nature". They are without hope without God. The 3 themes of the Bible story are coming together: God promises a Messiah (a Chosen or Anointed One) who will rescue his people so they can live with him.

The Messiah has been expected since Eden. God promised Eve a snake crusher from her descendants – someone to defeat sin and death. This Messiah will crush the devil but die in the process. God also promised to bless all the nations on earth through one of Abraham's descendants, and promised to rule his people from David's throne for eternity. The Messiah has a lot to do!

The prophets add to the expectation. God shows them glimpses of the Messiah's birth and death. This Chosen One will not be easy to miss. The New Testament tells how Jesus fulfils the prophecies, and how ironic it is that the religious leaders don't recognize him. He will be born in Bethlehem, David's hometown, born of a virgin, and will be God himself. This king will be perfect because he is not merely human.

The Messiah's death will bring about God's Rescue. Isaiah 53 shows how the Messiah carries the sin and suffering of his people, and heals them in turn. Since Eden, the punishment for sin is death, and the Messiah will take that punishment on himself. God's people continue to wait…

SCENE CARD

Binoculars: Prophets see in the future and promise a Messiah, a ruler who pays for sins.

CLOSE-UP

Isaiah's prophecy gives the best Old Testament picture of God's Rescue of all sinful people. He says, "We all, like sheep, have gone astray, each of us has turned to our own way; and the Lord has laid on him the iniquity of us all" (Isaiah 53:6). Humankind is helpless and wandering like sheep, but God plans to send one man to take their punishment and rescue them from sin.

FLASH-FORWARD >>>

The messianic prophecies point to events in the New Testament. Jesus rides into Jerusalem (Zechariah 9:9; Matthew 21:1–11). Judas Iscariot betrays Jesus (Psalm 41:9; Matthew 26:47–50). Jesus' clothes are divided up (Psalm 22:18; Matthew 27:35). Jesus dies with nothing (Daniel 9:26; Matthew 27:50). A black cloud of God's anger hangs over the land (Isaiah 53:6; Matthew 27:45).

BONUS FEATURES ✪✪✪

Did you know?

- *Isaiah made his prophecy about the ruler's death 700 years before Jesus. He writes in the past tense ("he carried… he was pierced… wounds have") because it was so certain to happen. People often speak the same way when an unfinished match is 100-0: "We have won!"*

ACTION PLANS

SCENE CARD

Binoculars: Consider how the prophets foretell a Messiah.

PRESENT BINOCULARS
(COMPARE WITH SIGNPOST).

- *Why might binoculars be better than signposts?*
- *Why does it help to have lots of people looking through binoculars?*

Discuss how Israel needs a faithful king and how God promised an eternal king to David. Discuss how the prophets gave lots of glimpses of the Messiah to see different things about him.

Word bank for 3-4 line summary:
prophets, Messiah, king, virgin, Bethlehem, dies, carry sin.

21 QUESTIONS

Play this "Guess Who" game to practise identifying people by their descriptions.

Discuss how the prophets played "Guess Who". Play 21 Questions: each child thinks of a famous person (alive/dead, fictional/real) and gives 3 clues about them. Try to identify them in fewer than 21 questions. Only yes/no questions! Alternatively, play it as a group game. Each group chooses someone and its members each reveal one clue. The guessing begins.

Review the exercise. How easy is it to "guess who"? What kinds of clues make it easier? Link to God's guessing game; he describes a Messiah coming in the future.

MORE GLIMPSES

Research further messianic prophecies.

What do these prophesy? Isaiah 35:5–6a; Psalm 72:10; Psalm 78:2; Psalm 16:10; Ezekiel 34:23–24. List the core of each, alongside the book's prophecies. Research more online – some say there are hundreds!

PICTURING THE PROPHECY

Identify a prophecy by a drawing or identify the drawing by the prophecy.

Read all of the prophecies and discuss their New Testament fulfilments. Children choose a prophecy and have 30 seconds to draw it. Others guess which prophecy they have drawn. Can they say the prophecy without reading it again?

Alternatively, address the prophecies one by one. Discuss the fulfilments and give the students 30 seconds to draw what they imagine. Play a 30-second countdown timer (YouTube) to jazz up the exercise.

DESIGNERS AND EDITORS

Draw, pass, and edit pictures of the Christmas and Easter prophecies.

Divide the students into 2 or 4 groups. Give each some large paper headed "Prophecies of birth" or "Prophecies of death". They have 2–3 minutes to begin pictures of the relevant fulfilments. Pass the pages: the next group writes the matching prophecy. Pass the pages: the next group labels the pictures. Pass the pages: the next group completes the drawings. Now everyone has worked on the birth/death prophecies twice.

Sheet: Messianic Matching Pairs

Play a matching game using prophecies and pictures.

Sheet: Prophecy Puzzle

Decipher what Isaiah foretold by arranging some phrases.

Read Isaiah 53:4–6. Don't give the interpretation about Jesus on the cross. Hand out the Prophecy Puzzle page. Children draw a line down the centre of their page and arrange the blocks as close to the line as possible. The boxes will form a cross. Children will need to place the two crossbeams side-by-side. Offer clues sparingly and stop early finishers giving the answer away!

Read Isaiah 53:4–6 again. Which words link to the cross? What is Isaiah foretelling?

ACT 6: THE PROMISED KING
SCENE 1: THE SON OF...

PRODUCTION NOTES

UNIT AIM

- *To see Jesus' titles and role on earth*

UNIT CONTENT

- *Jesus' family tree*
- *The Christmas story*
- *Jesus' baptism*

WIDE ANGLE: SETTING THE SCENE

The theme of God's Promises takes a new turn. In remote Bethlehem, a boy is born. Matthew calls him the "Son of Abraham, the Son of David, the Christ". Matthew immediately labels him as the promised king, the Chosen One who will rescue God's people. His name "Jesus" even means "the Lord saves" in Greek (the Hebrew equivalent is Joshua). God keeps his promises by fulfilling the prophecies about his birth: he is born in Bethlehem to a virgin.

The theme of Living with God also changes direction. Jesus is given many titles – Christ, Jesus, Immanuel – and Immanuel means "God is with us". John begins his Gospel about Jesus' life by saying that God makes his dwelling place among humans. God literally "tabernacles" with his people through Jesus (see page 40 on tabernacle). Jesus is the incarnation of God (God in the flesh), and God calls Jesus his "Son" at his baptism. God's rescue plan is in full swing.

SCENE CARD

DNA: A descendant of Abraham, David, and Son of God is born to live with humans.

CLOSE-UP

Jesus' baptism reveals his role and relationship with God. God's Spirit descends on Jesus like a dove to anoint him as *The Promised King* and Messiah, and a voice calls Jesus his Son. Jesus is the Messianic Son of God. Through Jesus, the people are *Living with God*.

FLASHBACK <<<

David was also born in Bethlehem. Jesus is called the "Son of David" because he descends from David and is the king promised to David. God's Spirit also anoints Saul and David as kings. The Spirit commissions them to rule, and commissions Jesus to rule for eternity.

BONUS FEATURES ✪✪✪

Did you know?

- *Christmas has pagan beginnings. The Romans celebrated "Saturnalia" during 17–23 December, a drunken feast worshipping the god Saturn and ending in human sacrifice. On 25 December they celebrated the Winter Solstice for the sun god Mithra. Constantine I, the first Christian emperor, moved Christmas to 25 December to replace these festivals, though the Gospels do not say when Jesus was born. Most scholars believe he was born sometime between 6 BC and 4 BC.*

- *Half a million people visit the site of Jesus' baptism each year, many wanting to be baptized where he was.*

ACTION PLANS

SCENE CARD

DNA: Consider Jesus' ancestors and titles.

PRESENT DNA.

- *What is DNA?*
- *Whose genes might be in Jesus' DNA?*
- *Why does it matter whom Jesus descends from?*

Discuss God's promises to Abraham and David – a descendant will bless the world, and rule the world for eternity. Recall what the prophets saw about the Messiah.

Word bank for 3-4 line summary:
Son of Abraham, Son of David, Jesus, Messiah, Immanuel, virgin, Bethlehem.

JUST A MINUTE

Play a quick game testing knowledge of Jesus' life.

Sort Jesus' life into categories. *The Blockbuster Bible* uses these: birth, friendships, miracles, teachings, death, and resurrection. For each category, children must explain what they know. Rules: no hesitation, repetition, deviation. Agree on time: try 30 seconds at first.

Alternatively, try it as a team game. Two teams challenge the speaker for inaccuracies, or hesitation, repetition, or deviation. They raise a hand to challenge. Points go to the challenger's team for correct challenges, or the opposition team for incorrect challenges.

JESUS HOT SEATING

Interview Jesus on aspects of his life.

The teacher plays Jesus – if you're confident on the details or willing to be exposed. Wear a costume item when in character. Children quiz the teacher on areas of Jesus' life, trying to catch the teacher out. Or the children play Jesus to answer each other's questions.

Alternatively, play a team game. Two teams write down questions to ask Jesus in turn. The teacher rates each question out of 5, and the opposition team rates the answer out of 5. Allow each team 3 or 4 questions and then gather scores.

Sheet: Big Claims

Rank claims made about Jesus.

Complete the sheet, or perform a ranking exercise. Review the quotations and sum them up together. Rank them in order of: size of claim, or surprise of claim. This is a tricky evaluation task, so summarize the quotations in a couple of words. Review: who else in history could compare to Jesus in each quotation?

Sheet: Family Tree Making

Sketch and design part of Jesus' family tree.

Sheet: ID Cards

Explain 6 different titles given to Jesus using The Blockbuster Bible.

Sheet: Cast and Crew

Perform the Nativity and repeat until it's right.

FLEXI-TASK

Photocopy and cut up the Cast and Crew sheet. Hand out the Director and Producer cards, and then the cast cards. Finish with remaining crew cards, if desired. Allocate the roles – children write down their part and what their character does.

Cast: Angel Gabriel, Mary, Joseph, Angel 2, Shepherd 1, Shepherd 2, Wise Man 1, Wise Man 2, Wise Man 3, King Herod, Chief Priest and Teacher 1, Chief Priest and Teacher 2.

Sit in a circle – acting in the middle. The cast perform the scenes, but the crew raise a hand at any time to pause the action and make corrections or suggestions. Actor's Understudies swap in for any actor when it's time for a change. Generate discussion on correct lines, actions, emotions, and creativity. Or perform the entire scene and then listen to the crew, starting with the Director.

Scenes: 1) Gabriel, Mary, Joseph; 2) Angel 2, Shepherds, Mary, Joseph; 3) Wise Men, Herod, Chief Priests and Teachers, Mary, Joseph.

ACT 6: THE PROMISED KING
SCENE 2: THE FRIEND OF SINNERS

PRODUCTION NOTES

UNIT AIM

- *To see how Jesus chooses his friends*

UNIT CONTENT

- *Jesus calls the first disciples*
- *Jesus calls Levi*
- *Jesus and the Samaritan woman*
- *Jesus and the Pharisees*

WIDE ANGLE: SETTING THE SCENE

By Jesus' time, many had lost sight of how to relate to God. Throughout the Old Testament God's people needed to trust him for forgiveness and acceptance. Abraham's faith was credited to him as righteousness, and even King David had to ask for forgiveness. Nobody was perfect. The Mosaic Covenant showed how to obey God, but also showed how far short they fell. Living with God depends on God accepting his sinful people when they ask for forgiveness. Jesus shows that anyone can live with God, no matter how sinful they have been.

Jesus surprised the religious leaders with his choice of friends. He chooses disciples (followers) from fishermen and tax collectors – *"Follow me!"* They drop their jobs and families in faith that following him is better. Even the worst in society are his friends. The difference is that they know they are the outcasts of society and don't deserve God's generosity. Levi is a prime example. The Pharisees (strict religious teachers) believe that only perfect people can live with God. Jesus attacks them for their hypocrisy – they don't practise what they preach. Jesus is a friend of sinners, but only some of the sinners. None are perfect. They must all submit to their king, but not all do.

SCENE CARD

Trash: Jesus gathers disciples who are often the outcasts of society and want forgiveness.

CLOSE-UP

God's Rescue comes to those who want a rescue. After Jesus calls Levi, the Pharisees ask why Jesus eats with tax collectors and sinners. But Jesus says only the sick need a doctor, not the healthy. He says he came not for the righteous but sinners. Jesus says he rescues those who want forgiveness, and tells the Pharisees they lead others to hell (Matthew 23:15).

FLASHBACK <<<

The 12 disciples echo the 12 tribes of Israel. Jesus calls together new people, and the 12 will just be the first of many. His new friends come from all over the world.

BONUS FEATURES ✪✪✪

Did you know?

- *The Pharisees were a sect of teachers demanding strict obedience to the Jewish Law. "Pharisee" comes from the Hebrew word for "separatists" or "separated ones". They clearly separated themselves from Gentiles and those who ignored the Law. The Pharisees opposed Jesus for how he taught his disciples and, though they wanted him dead, they played no part in the plot to arrest and put Jesus on trial.*

ACTION PLANS

SCENE CARD

Trash: Consider how Jesus chooses his friends from the lowest in society.

PRESENT TRASH.

- *Who should the Son of God choose as his friends?*
- *Why does he choose outcasts?*
- *How does he treat them like treasure?*

Discuss how trash represents the outcasts of society – sinners. Why might some think they are treasure? Discuss how some knew they were sinners, and others didn't. Why would Jesus treat the trash like treasure? Discuss how Jesus came to be their doctor, recycler, and friend.

Word bank for 3–4 line summary:
sinners, friends, fishermen, Peter, tax collectors, Pharisees, treasure.

Sheet: Cast and Crew

Perform the calling of the disciples and repeat until it's right.

Follow activity from "The Son Of..." on page 55. Allocate the roles and act out the scenes again and again.

Cast: Jesus, Simon Peter, Andrew, James, John, Zebedee, Levi, Roman Soldier, Eating Disciple, Pharisee 1, Pharisee 2.

Scenes: 1) Jesus, Simon Peter, Andrew; 2) Jesus, James, John, Zebedee; 3) Jesus, Levi, Roman Soldier, Eating Disciple, Pharisees.

Sheet: Gossip Column

Write some juicy gossip for a local magazine.

Discuss how Jesus shocked his audience. Use the Gossip Column sheet to create a magazine name and report the recent or exciting things the title character has apparently done, and on what others are saying about them.

Sheet: Furious Pharisees

As a Pharisee, write an angry response to Jesus' criticisms of you.

Sheet: Guess Who

Play "Guess Who" to recap Jesus' friends and enemies.

Print pages on card. List together Jesus' friends and enemies, and design a card for one person. Take turns to ask yes/no questions about your opponent's choice. If you guess a character, or if your opponent guesses incorrectly, you win.

Choices include: Gabriel, Mary, Joseph, Shepherds, Angels, Wise Men, King Herod, Chief Priests and Teachers, Simon Peter, Andrew, James, John, Zebedee, Levi, Pharisees.

Later choices include: Samaritan Woman, Servants, Paralysed Man, Lazarus, Martha, Mary (her sister), Bartimaeus, Demon-Possessed Man. Alternatively, use this with Old Testament characters, perhaps from 1 or 2 scenes.

Or play the party game version. Complete the cards, shuffle them, hand them out, and place them on foreheads. Children must identify themselves with the fewest questions.

FLEXI-TASK

FLEXI-TASK

ACT 6: THE PROMISED KING
SCENE 3: THE MAN OF SUPERPOWERS

PRODUCTION NOTES

UNIT AIM

- *To see how Jesus displays God's powers*

UNIT CONTENT

- *Miracles over nature*
- *Miracles over sin and sickness*
- *Miracles over death*
- *Miracles over demons*

SCENE CARD

Lightning Bolt: Jesus shows God's power over sickness, sin, death, nature, and demons.

CLOSE-UP

Jesus uses miracles to demonstrate he brings God's Rescue. He forgives the paralysed man because the man has faith, and because sin is the biggest problem facing people. He wants to forgive sins most of all. When the religious teachers challenge him, he heals the man to prove he can forgive. Forgiveness is the rescue that will bring people back to living with God.

FLASH-FORWARD >>>

Jesus' miracles foreshadow God's Rescue in the new creation. There is no suffering or death in heaven. The miracles show that God's kingdom has come because God's king has come.

BONUS FEATURES ✪✪✪

Did you know?

- *Jesus said, "I am the bread of life" just after feeding the 5,000. He said, "I am the light of the world" just before healing a blind man. He said "I am the resurrection and the life" just before raising Lazarus from the dead. He also said, "I am the Good Shepherd" some time before "laying down his life".*

WIDE ANGLE: SETTING THE SCENE

Jesus' miracles show who he is. The prophet Isaiah foretold a time when the blind will see, the deaf will hear, the lame will walk, and the mute will sing (Isaiah 35). When Jesus heals the sick, he proves himself to be God's Messiah. But this prophecy also points further into the future. Jesus' powers are a foretaste of God's kingdom in the new creation. Jesus is the promised king who will rule his people in eternity where there is no more death, mourning, crying, or pain. The miracles are not isolated incidents. They are signs of Jesus' eternal kingdom.

Living with God always had powerful results. In the Old Testament, God's people see miraculous things. God parts the Red Sea, stops the River Jordan, stops the sun in the sky, fills the tabernacle and Temple with the cloud of his glory, and raises the dead through his prophet Elijah. Jesus acts as a "new Elijah" – someone who demonstrates God's power. When he forgives the paralysed man his sins, he heals him to prove it. Jesus' powers show how he is God living with his people. He has power over sins, over sickness, over nature, over death, and over demons. Even though his powers sometimes scare the people, they should expect them when living with God.

ACTION PLANS

SCENE CARD

Lightning Bolt: Consider how Jesus uses God's powers.

PRESENT LIGHTNING BOLT.

- *How would God prove himself?*
- *What types of miracles did Jesus perform?*

Discuss which superpower the children would choose. Discuss how Jesus' powers fall into 5 categories – power over sickness, sin, nature, death, and demons. Discuss how Jesus served others with his powers, not like the Old Testament kings who served themselves.

Word bank for 3-4 line summary:
superpowers, Messiah, sin, sickness, nature, death, demons.

GUESS WHO

Play "Guess Who" to recap Jesus' friends and enemies.

See "The Friend of Sinners" for this activity (page 57). Add to the game the people met in this chapter.

BLIND BARTIMAEUS

Consider how blind Bartimaeus really was.

Discuss how "seeing" is another way of saying "believing". What does Bartimaeus believe, and how strongly? What do the crowd believe, and how strongly? What's the difference between Bartimaeus and the crowd? Spot how the crowd are blind and blind Bartimaeus sees. He calls Jesus "Son of David", God's promised king who rules for eternity.

Sheet: Mime Artists 2

Perform still poses for each of Jesus' miracles.

Equipment: *Camera, casting sheets, tape*

Discuss how pictures tell a story. Children mime the scenes of Jesus' miracles for a set of photos. Use the Mime Artists sheets and cast the roles for the scenes. Children write their character's expression. Work in groups of 8–10 or altogether. Give 2 minutes to rehearse their poses for their performance. Position the camera and lay out tape to mark the edges of the stage. Encourage good body language to capture actions and emotions. Show the photos back to the students.

Alternatively, or afterward, try it as a speed exercise. Time the group(s), taking photos when each pose is ready. Review how easy it was for Jesus to perform each miracle – what he did or said.

Sheet: Sorting Superpowers

Rank Jesus' powers in a few ways.

Hand out the Sorting Superpowers page for children to cut out each picture. The 6th picture is blank for children to fill in another miracle (e.g. walking on water/resurrection). Then rank the picture in a "Diamond 6". Make 3 rows of pictures: 1 2 3, 1 2, 1. This helps the children begin to justify their ranking without explaining. Rank in order of: most impressive, most want to witness, most helpful, most surprising, most important. Choose some categories, and get the children to write their reasons for their top 1. Why might power over sin be the most important?

Sheet: Newspaper Front Page

Write a newspaper story reporting on Jesus' miracles and superpowers in Galilee.

Sheet: Life Certificate

Complete a certificate to show how Lazarus came back to life.

ACT 6: THE PROMISED KING
SCENE 4: THE PREACHER OF PARABLES

PRODUCTION NOTES

UNIT AIM

- *To see what Jesus teaches his disciples*

UNIT CONTENT

- *The Lord's Prayer*
- *Parables about God's kingdom*
- *The Good Samaritan*
- *The Pharisee and the Tax Collector*
- *The Lost Son*
- *The Good Shepherd*
- *The Farmers*

WIDE ANGLE: SETTING THE SCENE

God's people need teaching. They believe that they are friends with God only if they obey him. But ever since the Passover and exodus, God shows that he rescues his people in order to live with them. They become friends because he makes them friends, not because they are perfectly obedient. Jesus' parables often show the difference between the two views. The parable of the Pharisee and the Tax Collector shows that God accepts the person who wants forgiveness, not the person who focuses on being perfect. There's a shocking reversal: God can accept even the worst in society and reject the best. The Lost Son shows the same. God is a generous God who accepts his people by faith alone.

Jesus also uses his teaching to explain God's Rescue. In the parable of the Good Shepherd, he promises to give up his life and to bring followers from another sheep pen. These will be Gentiles – non-Jews. Anyone across the world may live with God in his kingdom. In the parable of the Farmers, Jesus shows how it's the chief priests and teachers of the Law who will reject and kill him. Ironically, they know the story is about them and they go away and plot his death. The parable effectively leads to his death, and therefore God's Rescue. Mostly, though, the parables show God is gathering his people to live with them.

SCENE CARD

Teacher's Hat: Jesus teaches his disciples about God's kingdom and how God rescues his people.

CLOSE-UP

Parables are stories with deeper lessons. Jesus uses everyday objects and characters (seeds, nets, coins, Pharisees, tax collectors, farmers), and everyday settings (the Temple, fields, roads). He also uses twists to shock his audiences into new ways of thinking.

Many of the parables are about *God's kingdom*. *This* comes when human hearts submit to Jesus as king. But it will continue in the new creation when God's people will know and submit to him perfectly. God's kingdom is "both now and not yet".

FLASHBACK <<<

In the parable of the Good Shepherd, Jesus keeps using God's name for himself. At the burning bush, God calls himself "I AM". The Pharisees see this as another reason to plot to kill him. Their people's ancestors also rejected God's prophets such as Jeremiah, throwing him into a muddy cistern.

FLASH-FORWARD >>>

Jesus will include Gentiles (non-Jews) as his followers. In the Good Shepherd, Jesus says he will bring in sheep from another pen. Including Gentiles in the church will surprise many, especially Peter when the Roman Cornelius follows Jesus (Acts 10:34–35).

BONUS FEATURES ✪✪✪

Did you know?

- *Pharisees often exceeded the Law's requirements. Fasting was instructed once a week (not twice), and they should give 10 per cent of their crops (not everything). They even invented 39 new laws about the sabbath to avoid breaking the Mosaic law.*

ACTION PLANS

SCENE CARD

Teacher's Hat: Consider the ways Jesus taught his people.

PRESENT TEACHER'S HAT.

- *What makes a good teacher?*
- *Why are stories good ways of teaching?*
- *What might be Jesus' main lessons for his people?*

Discuss how Jesus taught using parables – picture stories with another meaning. Discuss how Jesus used normal, everyday pictures to teach (seeds, yeast, wheat, weeds, nets, farmers, weddings, etc.). Discuss how Jesus' friends – the sinners – follow his lessons, but his enemies the Pharisees will not.

Word bank for 3-4 line summary:
parables, God's kingdom, forgiveness, Pharisee and Tax Collector/Good Samaritan/Lost Son/ Good Shepherd/Farmers (explain one).

Sheet: Character Assessment and Hot Seating

Interview the Pharisee and the tax collector.

Equipment: *Paper and pens*

Recap the parable and interview the characters. Consider 3 aspects: body language, speech and tone, attitude to God and other people. Use the Character Assessment sheet. Choose an approach...

- Two groups each prepare both characters. They jot down ideas and nominate someone from each group to perform for a few minutes.
- Four groups each prepare one character.
- Pairs each prepare one character.
- Individual "method acting". Children work on their own and try to become the character and believe they are that person. Children are likely to perform the characters very differently. The teacher nominates the most in-character children to perform their method acting.

Sheet: Job Interview

Complete a job application for the role of Good Shepherd.

The answers need to be written in the first person, and the children can answer as Jesus or themselves. They can point out how they will be a great Good Shepherd, or possibly not the best one.

Sheet: Mime Artists 3

Perform still poses for the parable of the Farmers.

Equipment: *Camera, casting sheets, tape*

As in "The Man of Superpowers". Try to improve the quality of the activity: performing the poses more quickly and showing more expression in each pose. Review the activity, or photos: the owner's trust; the farmers' greed; the servants' faithfulness; the son's hopefulness.

Try creating your own Mime Artists sheet for the next unit – on Jesus' journey to Jerusalem, his death, and resurrection.

Sheet: Parable Writing

Write your own Good Samaritan parable.

Discuss the structure and the surprises of the Good Samaritan. It teaches how all people are neighbours to be loved, including those considered enemies by their society. Look at the story structure on the Parable Writing sheet and discuss the 4 elements of the Good Samaritan: characters and problem, surprising rejection, surprising helper, surprising generosity. Consider who would be the Samaritan today – someone disliked and rejected. Write a modern parable about how our impressions about people are wrong.

ACT 6: THE PROMISED KING
SCENE 5: THE SERVANT OF MANY

PRODUCTION NOTES

UNIT AIM

- *To see how Jesus dies to serve his people*

UNIT CONTENT

- *Jesus foretells his death and resurrection*
- *Jesus rides into Jerusalem*
- *The Last Supper and last prayers*
- *Jesus' trials, death, and resurrection*
- *Jesus appears to his disciples*

WIDE ANGLE: SETTING THE SCENE

The Bible story leads up to the cross. God's people have a problem with their sin, so God promises a snake crusher to defeat sin and death. In the Abrahamic Covenant, God promises to bless all nations on earth through one man. The Davidic Covenant promises a man to rule from David's throne for eternity. In the story of Holy Week, there are plenty of suggestions that Jesus is this king. He rides into Jerusalem while his people lay down palm branches as a symbol of victory. Roman soldiers mock him, dressing him in a royal purple robe and a crown of thorns, Pontius Pilate calls him the king of the Jews, and the religious leaders jeer that "if he's God's king, he will save them and himself". None of them realize that Jesus is completing God's Rescue through his death. These passages are filled with irony.

Jesus also sets an example the Old Testament kings never could. He is a humble, suffering king. He rides into Jerusalem on a donkey, not a war horse. He tells James and John that leadership is about service. He rescues his people by dying, not by fighting. His self-sacrifice is copied by God's people ever since. God's people expect a king who will defeat the Romans and re-establish Israel, but Jesus defeats humankind's great enemies: sin and death. He dies at Passover to remember God's Rescue in Egypt, but this rescue helps all humankind for all of time.

SCENE CARD

Crown of Thorns: Jesus rescues his people by being rejected by men and by God the Father, before rising from the dead.

CLOSE-UP

Four Cs explain *God's Rescue* here. (1) The Cloud covers the land for 3 hours and shows God's anger at sin. Jesus takes God's anger. (2) The Cry "It is finished" (John 19:30) shows Jesus has paid for sin. It means paid in full. (3) The Curtain in the Temple tears in two to give access to God. (4) The Centurion calls Jesus the Son of God. Only the centurion spots the signs – although ironically the others tell Jesus to come down from the cross "to save himself and us" (Luke 23:39).

FLASHBACK <<<

Jesus dies at Passover time as a Passover Lamb. The first Passover in Egypt pointed ahead to this worldwide Passover.

BONUS FEATURES ✪✪✪

Did you know?

- *The chief priests tried to pay the guards to say that the disciples stole Jesus' body while they were asleep (Matthew 28:11-15).*
- *Normally crucifixion took days; when the Romans wanted to speed up the process, they broke the criminals' legs. The term excruciating refers to pain "out of the cross".*
- *In Jerusalem, there are two possible resurrection sites. The Church of the Holy Sepulchre was established under Constantine I in the 4th century. The Garden Tomb was found in 1867 by a landowner digging cisterns. It stands near a rock face that looks like a skull (Mark 15:22) and was cut out of rock (15:46). It was made for 2 people but only one berth was finished and used. It supports the Gospels' account of how the rich man Joseph of Arimathea gave Jesus his tomb.*

ACTION PLANS

SCENE CARD

Crown of Thorns: Consider how Jesus suffers as a king.

PRESENT CROWN OF THORNS.

- *How is Jesus a king?*
- *How does Jesus suffer?*
- *What's ironic (or strange) about this?*

Discuss how the disciples wanted a warrior Messiah but got a servant Messiah. Discuss how Jesus died to defeat their greatest enemy (sin) and rose to prove it.

Word bank for 3-4 line summary:
Messiah, servant, warrior, donkey, crown of thorns, dies, rises.

CAST AND CREW

Perform how Jesus rode into Jerusalem and repeat until it's right.

Follow activity from "The Son Of…" (page 55). Allocate the roles and act out the scenes again and again.
Cast: Jesus, Disciple 1, Disciple 2, Donkey, Cloak-Layer, Branch-Layer, Crowd Leader, Crowd 1, Crowd 2, Pharisee 1, Pharisee 2, Pharisee 3.
Scenes: 1) Jesus, Disciples, Donkey; 2) Jesus, Disciples, Donkey, Cloak and Branch Layers, Crowds; 3) Jesus, Crowds, Pharisees.

PUT ON THE SPOT

Test a child on what the good news was.

Discuss the meaning of "gospel". What was the good news about the cross and resurrection? How did Jesus rescue people? (He carried God's anger against sin, paying the punishment and rising to prove it was complete.)

Children write 1–5 or 1–10 down their page and think of questions on what happened at the cross and the resurrection. Don't write the questions down. Nominate a child to face the students' questions; the teacher or children test them and each mark a tick, cross, or question mark for each answer. Whose question couldn't the child answer? Or whose question caught the group out with a wrongly marked answer?

Alternatively, all children write 3 questions: easy, medium, and hard. The students write E, M, H for each questioner and tick/cross a pupil's answers.

Sheet: Holy Week Timeline

Line up a timeline of events as quickly as possible.

Follow activity from "Warning and Hope!" (p. 51). Use the sheet arrange the events of Holy Week in order. Either use the same approach (of 4 options) to see improvement in the same activity, or choose a new approach.

Sheet: Questioning the King (Palm Sunday)

Complete the conversations that happened when Jesus rode into Jerusalem.

Sheet: Stage Directions

Complete the scene of Jesus' crucifixion using drawings, speech bubbles, and labels.

Sheet: The Promised King Crossword

Complete the crossword on Act 6 of The Blockbuster Bible (pages 98–139).

Sheet: Holy Week Snakes and Ladders

Test each other on knowledge of Jesus' way to the resurrection.

Discuss who supported and who opposed Jesus on his route to the cross. Write a list of supporters and enemies on the board: James, John, Peter, Disciples, Singing Crowds, Pharisees, Peter, Jewish Rulers, 1st Thief, 2nd Thief, Centurion, Joseph of Arimathea, Pontius Pilate, Nicodemus, Mary, Women. Play Snakes and Ladders in groups of 3–4. When children reach a snake or a ladder, they must ask each other a question on the unit to avoid going down or to earn going up. Keep questions possible, and interesting!

ACT 7: GLOBAL GOSPEL
SCENE 1: GO, GO, GO!

PRODUCTION NOTES

UNIT AIM

- *To see how Jesus sends his disciples*

UNIT CONTENT

- *The Great Commission*
- *The Ascension*
- *The Holy Spirit comes at Pentecost*

WIDE ANGLE: SETTING THE SCENE

God's Rescue is ready to go global. In the Old Testament, there were signs that many nations would enjoy God's blessing – the queen of Sheba benefitted from Solomon's wealth – but Jesus will now bless all nations on earth. The Abrahamic Covenant is about to affect all humankind.

The Great Commission is a fulfilment of the parable of the Good Shepherd. Sheep from another sheep pen will follow Jesus. His disciples must take the gospel (good news) to all nations and teach them to trust Jesus as God's rescuer, and then obey him. Like throughout the Bible, God's people can live with him only if they have faith. They don't have to be perfect to live with God. Jesus blesses them by living the perfect life and giving his perfect record to anyone who believes. He has risen from the dead to prove this. This good news goes global.

Pentecost reverses the effects of sin and death. At the Tower of Babel God mixes up the people's languages and scatters them. At Pentecost, Jesus sends the Holy Spirit to help the people understand even in their own foreign languages. The disciples speak in many tongues, and people from at least 15 countries understand the good news. On Pentecost 3,000 people believe the gospel. But Pentecost also points ahead to the new creation, where a great multicultural crowd gathers around God's throne. God's Rescue mission goes global.

SCENE CARD

Weather Vane: Jesus sends his disciples in all directions to teach good news about God's Rescue (the forgiveness of sins), and his Spirit lives in them to empower them.

CLOSE-UP

Jesus opens up *God's Rescue* to the world. He sends his disciples to Jerusalem, Judea, and Samaria – these stand for the local towns, the local regions, and the foreign countries. He promises the Holy Spirit to help them do this.

FLASHBACK <<<

God's Spirit commissions leaders in the Old Testament. Gideon, Samson, Saul, and David all did God's work with God's strength. Now the Spirit helps the disciples share the news of Jesus.

FLASH-FORWARD >>>

Jesus promises to be with them until the end of time, pointing ahead to his return as Judge.

BONUS FEATURES ✪✪✪

Did you know?

- *Jesus sent his disciples to all nations. The Joshua Project is a charity who estimate the spread of the gospel globally. They say there are approximately 17,000 people groups in the world. These are separate social groups with their own language and/or dialect. Approximately 40 per cent of these have not heard the gospel, working out to just over 3 billion people.*

- *The Holy Spirit's gift of speaking in a language unknown to the speaker is sometimes called "tongues". Paul speaks of this in 1 Corinthians 14.*

ACTION PLANS

SCENE CARD

Weather Vane: Consider how Jesus sent his disciples in all directions.

PRESENT WEATHER VANE.

- *What letters do these often use?*
- *What word do these make? [NEWS]*
- *What's the good news about Jesus?*
- *Where does the good news spread?*

Discuss how Jesus died to pay for his people's sin, and rose to prove it. Discuss how he wanted everyone to believe it, in all nations.

Word bank for 3–4 line summary:
gospel, Great Commission, spreads, all nations, Ascension, Holy Spirit, Pentecost.

NEWSPAPER EDITORS

Rank news stories to think about good news.

Equipment: *News cuttings*

Discuss why we like good news, and why it matters.

- How much are they good news?
- How surprising/important/relevant are they?
- Guess which were front-page stories.

Link this to good news about Jesus.
What had he done? Why? What will he tell his disciples to do?

JESUS SAYS

Play a game about following commands.

This is really "Simon Says". Option 1: the children obey when the teacher says, "Jesus says…". Try to catch people out, and link to obeying Jesus' commands. Discuss how Jesus commanded his disciples to be messengers across the world.

Or play "Jesus Says" to recap the scenes about Jesus. Give instructions Jesus gave, remembering the things Jesus said and did, while testing the children's reflexes! E.g. "Jesus says, 'Be baptized!'" "Jesus says, 'Get up and walk!'" "'Cast your nets on the other side!'"

Sheet: Headline Writing

Explore how headlines are written.

Look at some newspaper front pages (perhaps online). Discuss the English used: short sentences, catchy words, names and places, alliteration, use of colons. Extension: compare broadsheet and tabloid headlines.

As a group, create some headlines for the good news: e.g. "SIN IN THE BIN": miracle master Jesus pays price. "SURPRISING RISING": Jesus defeats death.

Use the sheet to write headlines for the events of "Go, Go, Go!" in *The Blockbuster Bible*.

Sheet: News Team

Prepare a news report on the Ascension and Pentecost.

FLEXI-TASK

Use the sheet to prepare roles of Newsreader, Interviewer, and Passer-by. Complete this as a group, where all children prepare each character, in groups of roles, or in groups of 3. Perform in front of the room for extra effect and drama. Present or project pictures of the events or backgrounds on the board or screen. Here are some suggestions for how to perform:

- Newsreader – sit and speak in deep voice
- Reporter – stand before background picture, use a microphone
- Passer-by – walk by and answer questions with shock and surprise

Alternatively, use the sheet to plan the speech.

ACT 7: GLOBAL GOSPEL
SCENE 2: NEW PREACHERS

PRODUCTION NOTES

UNIT AIM

- *To see how the disciples spread good news*

UNIT CONTENT

- *Peter preaches at Pentecost*
- *Peter meets Cornelius*
- *Stephen and Philip preach good news*
- *Paul meets Jesus and preaches good news*

WIDE ANGLE: SETTING THE SCENE

God recycles people with new power. The Bible story is full of weak people with good intentions. Without God's Spirit in the Old Testament, heroes like Abraham, Moses, and David still made mistakes. They lacked inner power. Only at times did God's Spirit strengthen people – think of Samson's or David's victories – but not to all believers everywhere. However, at Pentecost God sends his Spirit to all his people, and Peter stands up to explain the good news about Jesus' death and resurrection to thousands. Stephen later tells the chief priests and ruling council that Jesus is the Christ. They stone him to death. God transports Philip around to ensure the gospel spreads. God's people have a new inner power to obey him and share his message.

The gospel goes global largely through Paul. He is on his way to arrest Christians in Damascus when Jesus stops him and sends him to the Gentiles (non-Jews). He makes 3 missionary journeys, travelling about 8,000 miles around the Mediterranean, and writes at least 13 letters to the churches. It often shocks and confuses the Jews that God includes Gentiles among his people (Acts 11). Jesus' new preachers take God's Rescue global, even against persecution and opposition.

SCENE CARD

Recycled Sign: The Holy Spirit renews God's people and empowers disciples like Peter and Paul to tell the whole world about God's Rescue through Jesus.

CLOSE-UP

Peter's first sermon explains why the people should have expected *God's Rescue*. He quotes from the prophet Joel to say how God promised the Spirit to all people, and quotes from King David to say how God promised Jesus' resurrection. They should repent (turn back to God) and be baptized because God's rescue has finally come.

FLASHBACK <<<

Peter was not always prepared to speak in front of hostile crowds. At Jesus' trial, he denies knowing him 3 times. At Pentecost, he tells more than 3,000 people that they even killed him, all according to God's plan.

BONUS FEATURES ✪✪✪

Did you know?

- *Acts is the sequel to the Gospel of Luke, as he explains in Acts 1:1–4. He writes to Theophilus; this means "lover of God", which might refer to any believer.*

- *Acts 1:8 is a pattern for the whole book of Acts, when Jesus sends his disciples to Jerusalem, all Judea, and Samaria, and to the ends of the earth.*

- *All of the 12 disciples were either tortured, executed, or exiled, tradition has it. Tradition says Peter was crucified upside down in Rome. The Roman Catholic Church says his grave is under St Peter's Basilica in the Vatican City.*

ACTION PLANS

SCENE CARD

Recycled Sign: Consider how Jesus renews his disciples for better purposes.

PRESENT RECYCLED SIGN.

- *What needs recycling?*
- *How will Jesus renew his friends?*

Discuss how the trash of society know they need a rescue, and Jesus treats the trash like treasure. Discuss how Jesus reuses his people as messengers of the good news, and the Holy Spirit brings the good news to Gentiles (non-Jews).

Word bank for 3-4 line summary:
Holy Spirit, Peter, preacher, Pentecost, Christians, Saul (Paul), Gentiles (non-Jews).

CHILD PREACHERS

Perform Peter's first sermon with some audience participation.

Discuss how preachers preach. Compare to how teachers deliver messages and engage an audience at the sports pitch or in a hall. Give speaking challenges: how to play football/rugby/cricket; how to perform a musical instrument in a concert; how to behave when lining up for lessons.

Recap Peter's first sermon and the subject of each paragraph. Children could rewrite it briefly in their own words. Begin with "I'm not drunk!" and end with "You crucified God's king!"

Perform speeches to the group, keeping them short and snappy. The rest of the students could be the crowd responding together, "What shall we do?" The child playing Peter says, "Be baptized!" This is best done in a performance hall, meeting area, or church space, and using something like a pulpit or lectern. Some could be filmed.

CAST AND CREW

Perform Saul's conversion and repeat until it's right.

Follow activity from "The Son Of…" (page 55). Allocate the roles and act out the scenes again and again.

Cast: High Priest, Saul (Paul), Jesus, Servant 1, Servant 2, Judas, Ananias.

Scenes: 1) High Priest, Saul; 2) Saul, Servants, Jesus; 3) Saul, Servants, Judas; 4) Jesus, Ananias; 5) Ananias, Judas, Saul, Servants.

PAUL'S JOURNEYS AND LETTERS

Research where Paul sent his letters to.

Print off a map of the Mediterranean and plot where Paul travelled. Find a list of places online (perhaps be selective!). Then label where he sent letters to. He wrote to the churches in Rome, Corinth, Galatia, Ephesus, Philippi, Colossae, and Thessalonica. Discuss his commitment to spreading good news. His 3 missionary journeys covered roughly 1,400, 2,800, and 2,700 miles!

Sheet: Storyboarding Paul's Conversion

Complete a storyboard on the events of the story.

Sheet: Breaking News Screen

Complete the headlines for the local TV news.

FLEXI-TASK

Look at the Breaking News Screen template. Discuss possible text for the sections: location, news channel name, headline, subheading, scrolling text, quotes. Share the meanings of these sections:

- Headline – very short, even two words
- Subheading – one or two new details
- Scrolling text – two short phrases
- Quotes – dramatic and personal

The first could be done as a group. Encourage bad grammar for stronger groups – missing out unnecessary words like "the" and "and"; for example "man jumps into pool".

ACT 8: NEW CREATION
SCENE 1: NATION HUMANKIND

PRODUCTION NOTES

UNIT AIM

- *To see how God finally gathers his people*

UNIT CONTENT

- *John sees God fulfil his promises*
- *A great crowd live with God in the city*

WIDE ANGLE: SETTING THE SCENE

The 3 themes of the Bible story are finally at their end. God's people are Living with God. God's Promises are fulfilled. God's Rescue is complete. John has a revelation of the new creation where God reveals the new world that awaits his people. In it there is no sin or death, and Jesus wipes away every tear from his people's eyes. A great multicultural crowd gathers around the throne to worship him.

In his revelation, John sees people from all tribes, nations, and languages, wearing pure white clothes and waving palm branches. They are God's rescued people living with him.

The new creation comes after a delay. Jesus promises to judge the world with justice. If anyone's name is in the Lamb's book of life, they enter the new creation. The Lamb becomes the shepherd who rules his people in heaven – the shepherd king. He gathers his sheep and rules them from the throne. The delay until his coming allows time for the nations to trust and obey him, to join the guest list. But the delay is limited – Jesus will come unexpectedly like a thief in the night. The party gathering has a fixed start date. He just doesn't say when!

SCENE CARD

Happy People: In the new creation, God keeps his promises to Abraham and gathers all his people to live with him and worship him.

CLOSE-UP

The symbolism of the city shows its perfection. The 144,000 people symbolize the 12,000 believers from 12 tribes (Revelation 7:4–8). None are missing from the old creation. The 12,000 stadia (1,400 mile) cubic city reflects the city's perfection (21:16). The cubic shape resembles the Most Holy Place in the tabernacle. God will live there. The high wall and 12 gates symbolize absolute protection (21:12), while the gates that never close symbolize how there are no opponents left (21:25). The Lamb is the temple, where God's people will worship him perfectly (21:22).

FLASHBACK <<<

The new Jerusalem is unlike the Tower of Babel. The tower was built by people, for people. The city comes down out of heaven from God (21:2), and was made for them. God reunites the scattered nations around his throne.

BONUS FEATURES ✪✪✪

Did you know?

- *The book of Revelation contains lots of complex number symbolism. Often people say 3 represents God (the Trinity), 4 represents the whole earth (to its 4 corners), and 7 represents completeness and perfection (remembering the 7 days of creation).*

- *In Revelation 1:3 it says that anyone reading it is blessed, but in Revelation 22:18 it says that anyone adding to it will be cursed! The last word in the Bible is Amen.*

ACTION PLANS

SCENE CARD

Happy People: Consider how God gathers people from all nations in the new creation.

PRESENT HAPPY PEOPLE.

- *How does this fulfil the Abrahamic Covenant?*
- *How will God fulfil the Davidic Covenant?*

Discuss the Abrahamic and David Covenants – God will bless the world and rule the world through a descendant of Abraham and David. Discuss how the good news has helped people from all nations to enter the new creation.

Word bank for 3-4 line summary:
new creation, massive gathering, all nations, worship, Lamb, throne, white clothes.

HEAVEN'S QUESTIONS

Develop and rank questions on what makes heaven so perfect.

Generate some interesting questions on heaven and its main features. Hand out slips of paper and everyone writes their best question. Altogether, or in groups, rank the slips in order of children's interest. Which questions do the students want answered most? Can the children offer good answers? Read the chapter to answer some of the questions and discuss the rest afterward.

PASSAGE LOOKUP

Explore Jesus' return.

Equipment: *New Testaments*

Discuss the "day of the Lord", when Jesus promises he will return. When will he come? What will he do? Read Matthew 24:14 and 1 Thessalonians 5:1–3.

PROMISE FULFILMENT

Compare God's promises and fulfilment in heaven.

Write out summaries of the Abrahamic and Davidic Covenants. Separate the Abrahamic Covenant onto 3 lines – People, Land, Blessing. Then read 3D Freddie's interview with John, and write down the fulfilments next to the promises. This can be done on a whiteboard or in books, or on 2 sides of a card.

INTERVIEW READING

Grasp the tone of John's revelation.

Perform the interview with John, encouraging realism by varying the pace and volume and by using regular pauses. Pass a prop around such as an old-fashioned book/scroll to denote who is playing John. Write main lines on cards (children could put a logo on the back for fun).

Or perform it in groups of 4. Two act, one holds the camera, and the 4th is the script supervisor. Give a time limit and film them if possible.

Sheet: Postcard from Heaven

Write a postcard about the new creation using John's Revelation.

Sheet: Home Sweet Home Picture

Create a group picture of heaven by passing it around.

Children draw the features of heaven according to John's Revelation. Give 2–3 minutes before passing their pages onto other pairs to complete, change, and add to the work. Repeat the passing 3 or 4 times, or until the exercise has served its purpose. The first pair should name their sheet, and pairs should label the features.

Or work in pairs without passing between groups. One child dictates and the other draws. Alternatively, work as individuals.

ACT 8: NEW CREATION
SCENE 2: GOD'S NEW EDEN

PRODUCTION NOTES

UNIT AIM

- *To see how God's people reign in the new creation*

UNIT CONTENT

- *God makes a new and better Eden*
- *Humans reign forever with God*
- *Jesus promises to return to earth*

WIDE ANGLE: SETTING THE SCENE

John's vision closes with a picture of restoration. The Garden of Eden is now a garden city. Humans live with God again with restored roles. In the new Eden, they rule alongside Jesus, sharing in his victory over sin and death. It's a restoration and a celebration! God's Rescue has made them in the likeness of God (like in Genesis 1), and made them rule as kings alongside Jesus. They have equal status with Jesus.

The final words call for Jesus to return. Jesus calls himself the bright morning star. A morning star signals that dawn is coming. Jesus signals that the eternal dawn is coming. He is the Root and Offspring of David – David's creator and descendant. He is the king who rules God's people for eternity. The dawn is eternal because they can eat from the tree of life once more – another picture of restoration. God's people wait for his coming because it begins an eternity where the Bible's 3 themes are combined: humans are Living with God, God's Promises are fulfilled, and God's Rescue is complete. It's a wrap!

SCENE CARD

The Tree of Life: God's people live with God forever and reign as kings, after Jesus promises to return as Judge.

CLOSE-UP

God restores his rule and blessing in the new Eden. The river and the tree of life symbolize restored eternal life and paradise (22:1–2). God sits on the throne and lifts the curse of death (22:3). Humankind moves from tending the garden to ruling the city with their king for ever and ever (22:5). They will submit to God's rule and enjoy his blessing for eternity. This new state is permanent.

FLASHBACK <<<

The landmarks in Revelation 22 deliberately echo those in Genesis 2. The river flowing through the city and the tree of life promise paradise and eternal life for those living there (22:1–3).

BONUS FEATURES ✪✪✪

Did you know?

- *Jesus called himself "the Alpha and the Omega" in the first and the last chapters of Revelation (1:8 and 22:13). They are the first and last letters of the Greek alphabet.*

- *The Eden Project in Cornwall, UK, is also a symbol of regeneration and restoration. It turned a clay pit into paradise and is now a visitor attraction and educational charity. "Eden" means "delight" and first appears in Genesis 2.*

ACTION PLANS

SCENE CARD

The Tree of Life: Consider how God's people live forever in a renewed Eden.

PRESENT THE TREE OF LIFE.

- *What does the Tree of Life do?*
- *Why can God's people eat from it again?*

Discuss how God's people live with him in the new creation, and how they can live forever. Discuss how the tree of life heals the nations, and they can't sin again. They serve God as kings.

Word bank for 3-4 line summary:
new Eden, tree of life, heals, throne, river, reign, return.

MOVING HOUSE

Discuss what makes a good home.

Ask questions about what we'd keep about our home if we had to move house. Size, layout, position? People there or nearby? Anything else? Link to heaven – what might God keep in his new Eden?

COMPARING EDENS

Draw pictures of each Eden and compare the features.

Read the Polaroids about the Edens and compare with the Garden of Eden in the chapter "Living with God". Discuss the links. The children then work in pairs, groups, or as individuals to draw pictures of each Eden – one per sheet. When drawing God, draw his shadow or a bright light.

Play Spot the Difference. Children hold up one picture and challenge others to guess which Eden they have drawn. Then children label their pictures carefully.

VERBAL TENNIS

Play a word association game on the two Edens.

Discuss the differences between each Eden, listing some keywords about each. Children sit in pairs opposite each other and say a keyword back and forth at each other. Each player uses words from a different Eden. Scoring like tennis: 15–love, 30–love, 30–15, 40–15, game. Rules: no repeats in the same point, no hesitating, umming, erring, or deviating.

E.g. (1) "Tree of the knowledge of good and evil" (2) "Tree of life" (1) "River Tigris!" (2) "Crystal clear River!" (1) "Animal helpers!" (2) "Lamb on the throne!" (1) "Adam and Eve" (2) "Umm!" (1) "Point to me! 15–love."

Play best of 3 games. Avoid using the same words in a game/consecutive games.

Sheet: Sorting Sentences 2

Sort 5 descriptions without talking.

Here's another way to use the Sorting Sentences sheet. In groups of 3–4, children cut out the 15 boxes and lay them face up on the table. Jumble them up and each take a roughly equal share. They should make 3 lines of 5 boxes to recreate the promises.

Rules: no talking and no taking. No demanding and no refusing. Children must look for who needs their spare phrases. Relax the rules if it's too challenging. Alternatively, the boxes could remain in the middle of the table and children take them one by one.

Sheet: Tourist Brochure

Design a brochure that "sells" the new creation.

Use the chapters "Nation Humankind" and "God's New Eden" to form an idea of the "selling points" of heaven. Discuss together what's perfect about the 3 aspects of the new creation. Think together of some tag lines.

FLEXI-TASK

Sheets: Theme Roundups 1-3

Summarize the Bible story according to the 3 themes: Living with God, God's Promises, and God's Rescue.

Sheet: Scene Cards

Arrange the 24 scene cards in order, remembering key characters and stories.

Cut out and sort these boxes into categories. Work out what links them and be ready to explain your reasons. Write a word below each number to describe what it is about, e.g. authors, years, AD. Use p. 6–7 of *The Blockbuster Bible* to help you.

1,600 -------------------	**PROPHECY**	**LIBRARY**	**100** ----------------------
SONGS	**REVELATION**	**27** ----------------------	**MOSES**
40 ----------------------	**PROVERBS**	**LAW**	**NEW TESTAMENT**
HISTORY	**JESUS**	**KINGS**	**TORAH**
ISRAEL	**OLD TESTAMENT**	**POETRY**	**39** ----------------------
LETTERS	**PROPHETS**	**GOSPELS**	**1500** ----------------------

TRIVIA CARDS

FLEXI-TASK

Quiz your classmates! Cut out the 2 cards, fold them down the middle, and write your questions. Write a topic to gather questions on a similar thing.

Topic:

Questions:

Answers:

Topic:

Questions:

Answers:

COMPLETE THE CLAPPERBOARD

You are filming a famous scene from the Bible story. Record the details to help the crew understand what's happening.

FILM TITLE:

SCENE: **CHARACTERS:**   **PROPS:**

PLOT:

Production Notes

Key moment of the scene:

_____

_____

_____

Why this scene is important:

_____

_____

_____

Make a VIP card for humankind using the word bank at the bottom of the page.

VIP

Name:

Jobs:

Draw:

PHOTO

Important because:

ACCESS ALL AREAS

image   *male*   *female*   *different*   *blessed*   *rulers*   *increase*   *plants*   *very good*

HUMANS

Write an acceptance speech for VIP Humankind. Everyone has VIP Status!

Use creative language: avoid "good/bad/happy/sad", and show your emotion all the way through. Use p.12–13 of *The Blockbuster Bible* to help you.

VIP HUMANKIND

Thank you! This means so much to me!

Getting this award makes me feel...

_____

_____

God told us our position in the world. He said...

_____

_____

There are so many reasons why humankind is special...

_____

_____

Our jobs have been to...

_____

_____

God blessed us to...

_____

_____

So, I just want to thank...

_____

_____

_____

BLUEPRINTING

Create a blueprint of the Garden of Eden using these pictures. Cut them out and stick them onto graph paper. Label the characters. Then design the scene around them.
If you have time, add more of your own, but do not draw God. Write speech bubbles for what each character says. God can speak from the side of the picture.

Design: "Living with God"

Adam

Eve

Tree of knowledge of good and evil

Tree of life

Other trees

Precious stones

River dividing into 4

Lion

Dog

Gorilla

Gold

Horse

You are Adam in the Garden of Eden. Describe what happened between you, God, the animals, and Eve. Use p. 14–15 of *The Blockbuster Bible* to help you.

FRIENDSHIP STATUSES

FRIENDS WITH GOD

My birth:
God moulded me from the ground and breathed into my nostrils

My one rule:

My job:

FRIENDS WITH ANIMALS

My problem:

My helpers:

My naming:

FRIENDS WITH WOMAN

My problem:

My helper:

My wife:

FIXING THE FALL

Recreate the Fall by cutting up these pictures and putting them back together, in story order. How fast can you do it? There are 8 pictures. Use p. 16–17 of *The Blockbuster Bible* to help you.

When you finish, give each picture a title and some captions.

Storyboard how Adam and Eve turned their back to God and write their speech below. Add extra labels like in box 1. Use p. 16–17 of *The Blockbuster Bible* to help you.

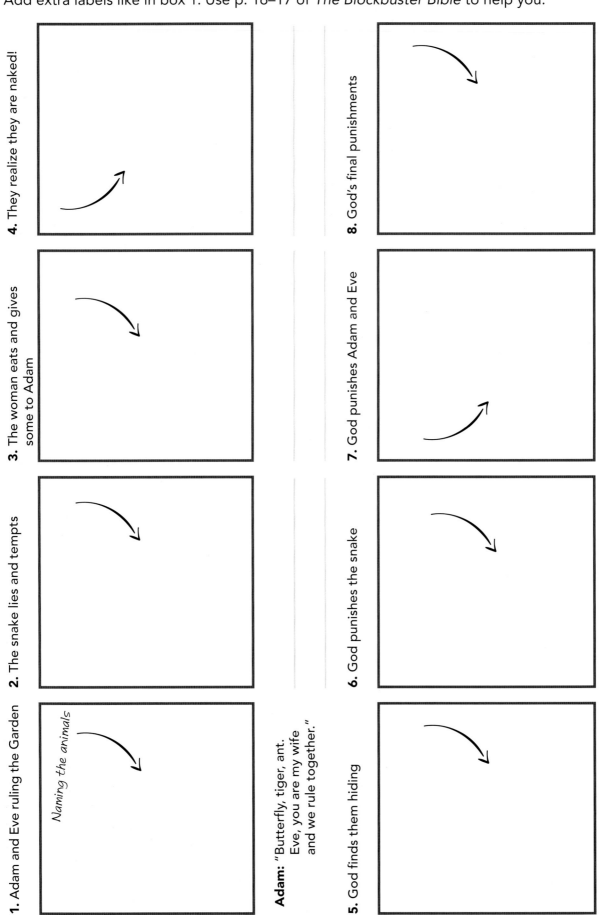

4. They realize they are naked!

3. The woman eats and gives some to Adam

2. The snake lies and tempts

1. Adam and Eve ruling the Garden

Naming the animals

Adam: "Butterfly, tiger, ant. Eve, you are my wife and we rule together."

8. God's final punishments

7. God punishes Adam and Eve

6. God punishes the snake

5. God finds them hiding

SIN AND DEATH SPREAD

Cut out the 4 main boxes and stick them down your page, then fill them in without sentences (see example). Grace is God's undeserved generosity. Use p. 18–21 of *The Blockbuster Bible* to help you.

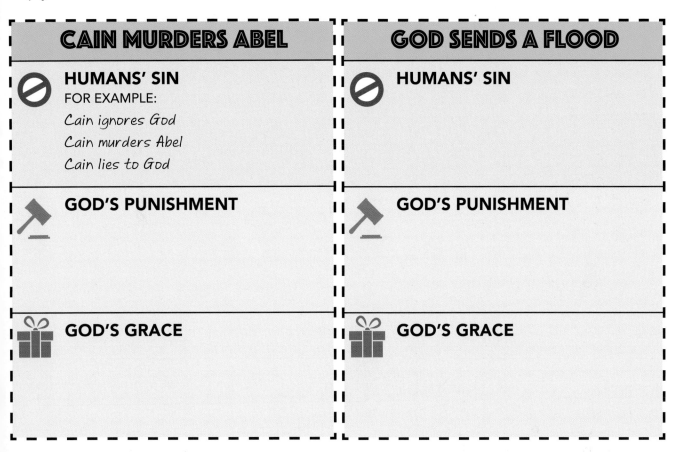

CAIN MURDERS ABEL

HUMANS' SIN
FOR EXAMPLE:

Cain ignores God

Cain murders Abel

Cain lies to God

GOD'S PUNISHMENT

GOD'S GRACE

GOD SENDS A FLOOD

HUMANS' SIN

GOD'S PUNISHMENT

GOD'S GRACE

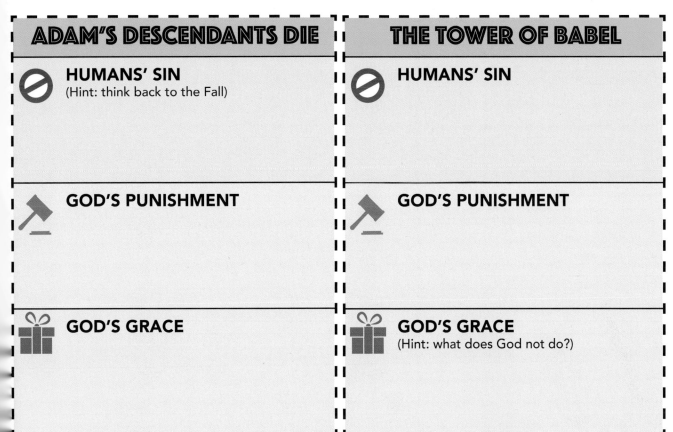

ADAM'S DESCENDANTS DIE

HUMANS' SIN
(Hint: think back to the Fall)

GOD'S PUNISHMENT

GOD'S GRACE

THE TOWER OF BABEL

HUMANS' SIN

GOD'S PUNISHMENT

GOD'S GRACE
(Hint: what does God not do?)

STORYBOARDING

FLEXI-TASK

Storyboard a scene by writing titles for each shot above the pictures, drawing the shots, and writing the speech. Label the pictures as you go.

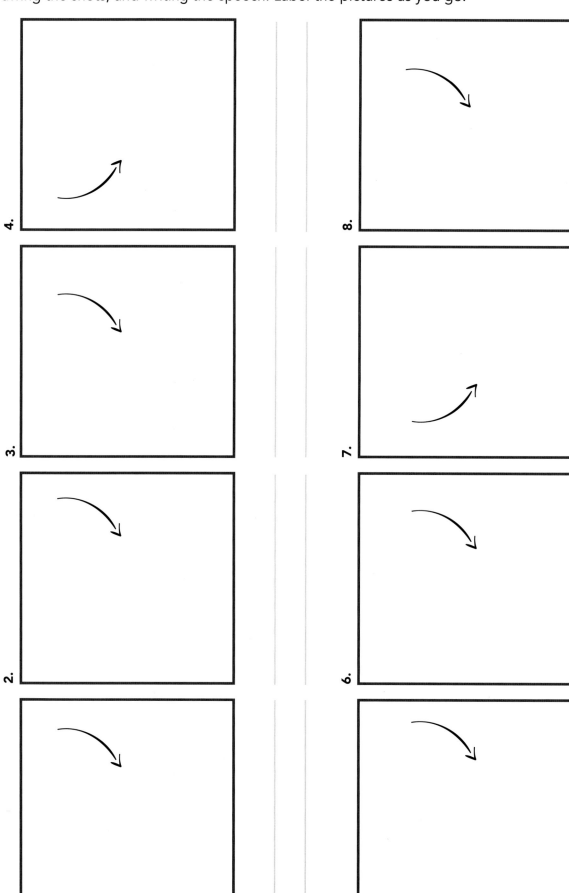

COVENANT CATEGORIES

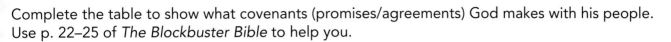

Complete the table to show what covenants (promises/agreements) God makes with his people. Use p. 22–25 of *The Blockbuster Bible* to help you.

	Promise to whom? Read carefully!	**Promise about...**	**Promise reminder is...**
Noahic Covenant	------------------------- ------------------------- ------------------------- ------------------------- -------------------------	God promises never to flood the world again.	------------------------- ------------------------- ------------------------- ------------------------- -------------------------
Abrahamic Covenant	------------------------- ------------------------- ------------------------- ------------------------- -------------------------	------------------------- ------------------------- ------------------------- ------------------------- -------------------------	God tells Abraham to circumcise his son and all his male descendants to remind them that God has made them different.
Mosaic Covenant	------------------------- ------------------------- ------------------------- ------------------------- -------------------------	------------------------- ------------------------- ------------------------- ------------------------- -------------------------	------------------------- ------------------------- ------------------------- ------------------------- -------------------------
Davidic Covenant	------------------------- ------------------------- ------------------------- ------------------------- -------------------------	------------------------- ------------------------- ------------------------- ------------------------- -------------------------	NONE

Complete the crossword about God's covenants.
Use capital letters and a pencil in case you're wrong! Use p. 22–25 of *The Blockbuster Bible* to help you.

ACROSS

4 What Israel should do on the sabbath. (4)

5 The third covenant after Eden. (6)

7 Israel was promised to be this. (7)

9 One of Abraham's descendants will crush this. (5)

10 God's covenant about a King of Kings. (7)

11 God promised this to Abraham. (4)

14 Where God makes one of his covenants. (5,5)

15 God bases his covenants on these. (8)

16 Abraham would lead a great… (6)

18 The second covenant after Eden. (9)

19 God promised to give this thirdly to Abraham and his descendants. (5)

DOWN

1 Abraham means "… of many". (6)

2 God promised Abraham a nation of… (6)

3 A promise receiver. (5)

6 Something that helps people remember God's promises. (8)

7 The reminder for Israel. (7)

8 This ring helps to remember God's promises. (5)

12 The serious promises or agreements between God and his people. (9)

13 One covenant reminder/sign. (7)

17 The first covenant after Eden. (6)

COVENANTS TIMELINE

Make a timeline to show how the Bible story begins. Stick the line across the middle of your page (landscape), and lay out the events and covenants in order, above and below the line. Draw marks with a ruler to connect them to the line. Use p. 22–25 of *The Blockbuster Bible* to help you.

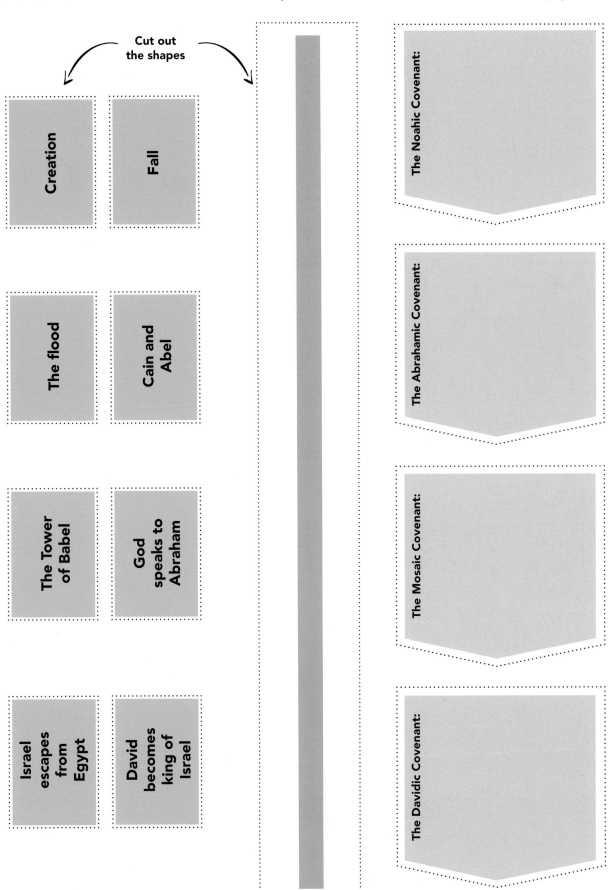

Cut out the shapes

Creation

Fall

The flood

Cain and Abel

The Tower of Babel

God speaks to Abraham

Israel escapes from Egypt

David becomes king of Israel

The Noahic Covenant:

The Abrahamic Covenant:

The Mosaic Covenant:

The Davidic Covenant:

FLEXI-TASK

Record a story's main details as a promo poster. Impress the reader!
Draw a picture in the space and colour it in.

Cast

Makers

Movie title

Catchy tag line

Review 1

Review 2

Release date

Cut out and organize God's 3 promises to Abraham. Each one has 5 boxes. When you are finished stick them into your book and draw symbols for each of the promises, trying to sum up the whole meaning of the promise. Use p. 26 of *The Blockbuster Bible* to help you.

go to the land	I will bless you	into a great
children as the stars.	nation on	Abraham,
nation of people.	I will show you.	earth through you.
I will bless every	You will have as many	country and
leave your	I will make you	and make you famous.

Perform the scenes with still poses. Circle your character and plan your expression using the word bank for ideas. Stay the same character throughout. Use p. 29-35 of *The Blockbuster Bible* to help you.

THE LIVES OF THE PATRIARCHS (FATHERS OF ISRAEL)

SCENE 1: Abraham sacrifices Isaac

Abraham is willing to sacrifice **Isaac** on an altar. An **angel** calls stop!

They find a **ram** caught in a bush. EXPRESSION: _____

SCENE 2: Abraham's servant finds a wife for Isaac

Abraham sends his **servant** to find a wife for **Isaac**. He has **camels**.

He finds **Rebekah**, who lives with her **parents**. EXPRESSION: _____

SCENE 3: Isaac prays for sons

Isaac prays to God for **Rebekah** to have a son. She gives birth to two sons –

Jacob and hairy **Esau**. They have **servants**. EXPRESSION: _____

SCENE 4: Jacob buys the birthright

Jacob buys from **Esau** the right to be next chief. He pays a bowl of soup!

They have **servants** and **goats**. EXPRESSION: _____

SCENE 5: Jacob marries two women

Jacob marries **Rachel** at last, after **Uncle Laban** tricked him into marrying his older

daughter, **Leah**. There are **wedding guests** and **servants**. EXPRESSION: _____

SCENE 6: Jacob wrestles God

Jacob wrestles with **God**, who pops his hip out of joint. EXPRESSION: _____

SCENE 7: Isaac prays before meeting Esau

Jacob is returning home and prays to God that **Esau** will no longer be angry.

He brings with him **sons** and **servants**. EXPRESSION: _____

agony   shock   compassion   relief   anger   desperation   confusion
blankness   trickery   love   worry   delight   calmness   jealousy

Tell a story with a few snapshots. Title each section of a person's life and write fun comments showing how the person feels about their memories.

JOURNEY MAPPING

Present the journey from Egypt to the desert. Cut out all the shapes and place the map in the middle of your page. Then write in more bits of speech. Last, arrange the speech in the correct order. Use p. 42–43 and 48–50 of *The Blockbuster Bible* to help you.

12 spies:
We were like grasshoppers compared to the people.

Israel:
Let's go back to Egypt and have a new leader.

Moses:
Go and spy out our land. See who lives there… Bring back some fruit…

Moses:
People of Israel, tomorrow we leave! Let us follow the Lord!

The Lord:
I am the Lord who rescued you. I will meet with you.

The Lord:
They will wander in the desert for 40 years.

Moses:
The Lord says, "The Egyptians will see my glory!"

Joshua and Caleb:
The land is ours for the taking. God promised it!

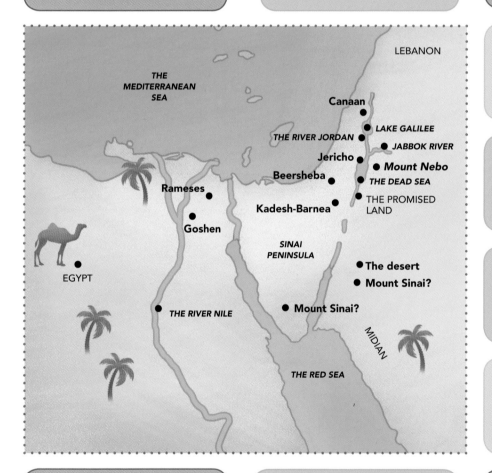

Report how God rescued the Israelites from slavery and brought them to freedom. Use reporter styles like "reports say", or "eyewitnesses…". Use p. 40–43 of *The Blockbuster Bible* to help you.

 # THE EGYPTIAN SUN

Sum up the whole story with a headline:

The Israelites' situation: *For 400 years, we lived…*

_____
_____
_____
_____
_____
_____
_____

Picture:

Picture caption:

The Burning Bush:

_____
_____
_____
_____
_____
_____

The Passover:

_____
_____
_____
_____
_____
_____

The Ten Plagues:

_____
_____
_____
_____
_____

The Exodus:

_____
_____
_____
_____
_____

EXODUS SNAKES AND LADDERS

Follow Moses and the Israelites from captivity to freedom. Careful you're not caught by Pharaoh and his slave drivers!

At a snake or ladder, answer your classmates' question to avoid sliding down, or to climb up!

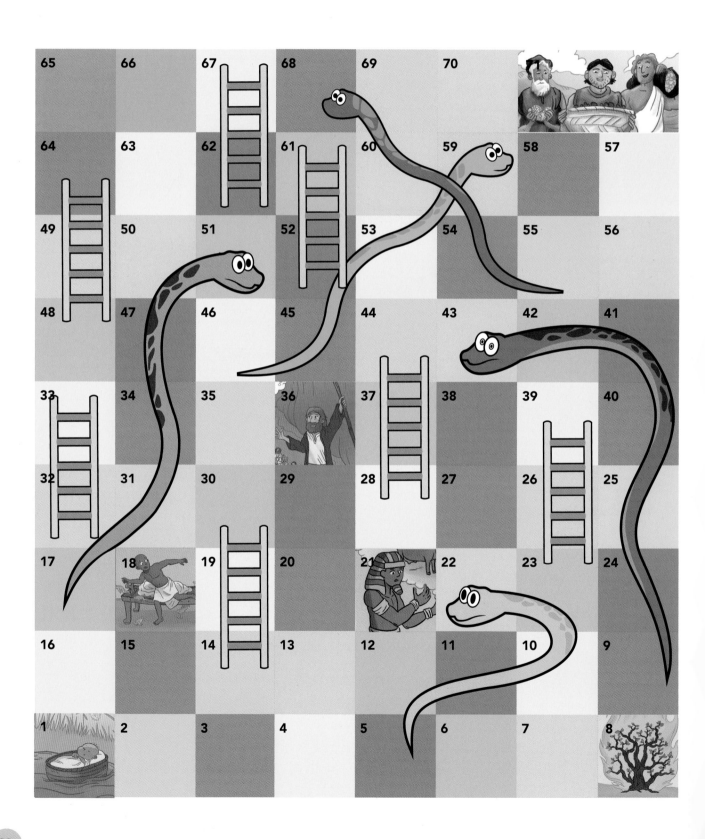

TABLET FOR LIVING

Complete this tablet with God's reasons for the Law, the tabernacle, and the sacrifices.
Then draw and colour a picture to symbolize them. Use p. 44–47 of *The Blockbuster Bible* to help you.

Why the Law is special...

_____

_____

_____

_____

Picture

Why the tabernacle is special...

_____

_____

_____

_____

Picture

Why the sacrifices are special...

_____

_____

_____

_____

Picture

Complete the 4 gift cards with descriptions for God's gifts. Then design the picture for the back, with a catchy tag line. Use p. 44–47 of *The Blockbuster Bible* to help you.

 **LAW**

This gives the bearer:

Tag line: *New laws for holy lives.*

 **MANNA AND RUNNING WATER**

This gives the bearer:

Tag line:

 TABERNACLE

This gives the bearer:

Tag line:

 **SACRIFICES**

This gives the bearer:

Tag line:

Make God's tent in 3D. First complete the blanks. Then build on the paper in groups, using stationery or play dough. The best one wins the "Michelangelo Sculpture Prize"! Use p. 46 of *The Blockbuster Bible* to help you.

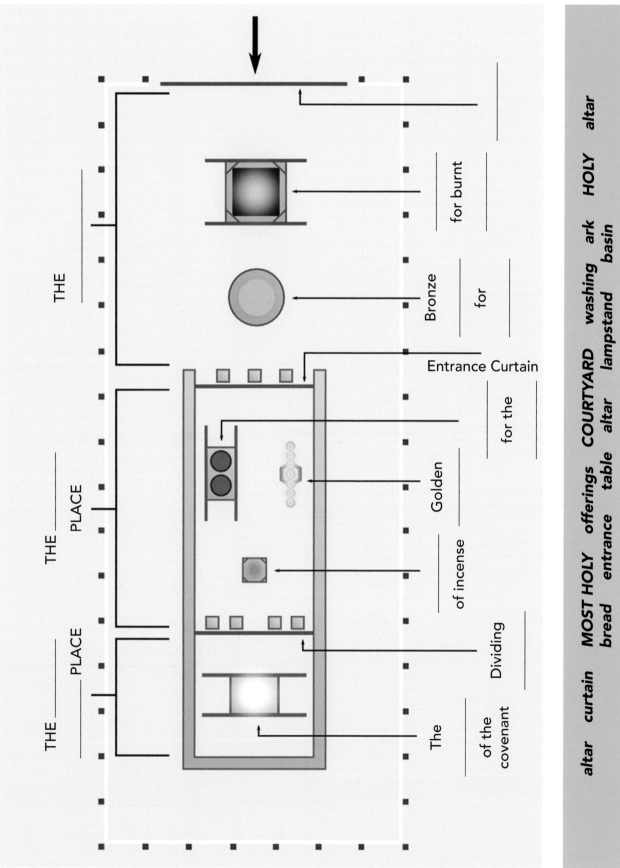

THE _____

_____ for burnt _____

Bronze _____ for _____

THE _____ PLACE

THE _____ PLACE

Entrance Curtain

_____ for the _____

Golden _____ of incense

Dividing _____

The _____ of the covenant

altar   curtain   *MOST HOLY*   *offerings*   *COURTYARD*   *washing*   *ark*   *HOLY*   altar
         bread   entrance   table   altar   lampstand   basin

Show how the Israelites felt on their way to the Promised Land. Plot a line graph, write a describing word by each point, then draw pictures above. Use p. 48–50 of *The Blockbuster Bible* to help you.

Picture Summary…	Good feelings…	Bad feelings…

Timeline (bottom axis, left to right):

- Israel leaves Mount Sinai
- They reach the Promised Land.
- Moses chooses and sends out 12 spies.
- Spies return; describe land and fruit.
- They describe the inhabitants and their cities.
- Joshua and Caleb tell them to trust God.
- Israel rebels; God sends them to wander desert.
- Israel complains about manna and quail.
- God sends poisonous snakes; many die.
- Moses prays; God saves by the bronze snake.

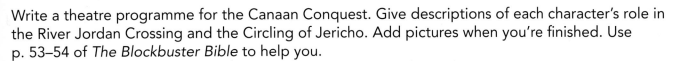

CONQUEST CAST LIST

Write a theatre programme for the Canaan Conquest. Give descriptions of each character's role in the River Jordan Crossing and the Circling of Jericho. Add pictures when you're finished. Use p. 53–54 of *The Blockbuster Bible* to help you.

CHARACTER DIRECTIONS

River Jordan Crossing

Priests: _____

_____

Soldiers: _____

People of Israel: _____

Joshua: _____

_____

_____

God: _____

_____

_____

Circling of Jericho

Priests: _____

_____

Soldiers: _____

People of Israel: _____

Joshua: _____

_____

_____

God: _____

_____

_____

SCRIPTWRITING

Write a play script and stage directions for a dramatic scene.
Perform it when you're ready!

Setting: _____ Scene name: _____

_____

(Character) :   (Stage direction)   (Speech)

_____   _____

                       _____

_____   _____

                       _____

_____   _____

                       _____

_____   _____

                       _____

_____   _____

                       _____

_____   _____

                       _____

_____   _____

                       _____

_____   _____

                       _____

_____   _____

                       _____

_____   _____

FLEXI-TASK

Choose a scene or group of scenes. Describe the content that gives it an 18 rating.

THE BIBLE BOARD OF FILM CENSORS

This is to certify that

Film's title:

has been classified for Cinema Exhibition

Sign here

PRESIDENT

Description of violence/bloody bits:

The film includes…

In one scene…

There is another scene where…

One character…

At the end…

18

Sign here

DIRECTOR

ACCEPTANCE SPEECH (BEST JUDGE)

Imagine you are a Judge. You have won the Best Judge award.

Tell how you led Israel, and show your personality: Ehud is brave; Deborah is wise; Gideon is weak; Samson is arrogant. Use p. 56–59 of *The Blockbuster Bible* to help you.

BEST ....

Wow! I can't believe... _____
_____
_____

Do I deserve this award? Well... _____
_____
_____

Our enemy was the... _____
_____

Here's how I led Israel... _____
_____
_____
_____
_____
_____

Our victory happened when... _____
_____
_____
_____

So, I just want to thank... _____
_____
_____
_____

Complete the conversation with David and Solomon. Make it as real as possible and use lots of facts while you speak. Use p. 64–70 of *The Blockbuster Bible* to help you.

You: How did you beat that giant? He was 3 metres tall!

You: Why didn't you kill Saul when you had the chance?

David: _____

David: _____

You: _____

You: _____

David: The ark shows that God is king above me. No! He's the true king of Israel!

David: It's the Davidic Covenant. God promised to make an eternal king from my family line.

You: Why did you choose wisdom? You could have asked for anything!

You: So why did God give you wealth?

Solomon: _____

Solomon: _____

You: _____

You: _____

Solomon: It replaced the tabernacle and God filled it with a cloud.

Solomon: Because I felt like it! I can marry who I want! I can do what I want!

Look up answers in God's Judges and God's Kings in *The Blockbuster Bible*. Complete the crossword with capital letters. Use a pencil in case you're wrong!

ACROSS

6 The lady who hammers a tent peg through the Canaanites army commander's head. (4)

7 The leader of a 300–man army. (6)

8 The lying wife of an unfaithful Judge. (7)

10 The queen who marvels at Solomon's kingdom. (5, 2, 5)

12 This man anoints Saul and David as king. (6)

13 How Gideon felt when he fought the Midianites. (4)

15 The fat king of Moab stabbed by Ehud. (5)

16 This was the secret to Samson's strength. (4)

17 The thuggish leader who battled the Philistines. (6)

DOWN

1 The first king of Israel. (4)

2 Solomon asks God for this. (6)

3 A left-handed Judge. (4)

4 The wife of Uriah, who David makes pregnant. (9)

5 Samson used this to kill 1,000 Philistines. (7)

6 Saul's son and David's closest friend. (8)

7 A 3–metre tall man who challenges Israel's God. (7)

8 This lady supported and advised Barak on beating the Canaanites. (7)

9 David wants to build this for God, but Solomon does. (6)

11 The type of women that Solomon wrongly marries (7)

14 The name of David's father. (5)

PLAYING CARDS

Complete a card describing any character. Score them under 6 categories (out of 100) and include a short biography about their highs and lows. Then draw their lifetime highlight.

Face:

Name:

Picture of a lifetime highlight:

POWER	/100	WISDOM	/100
LEGENDARY STATUS	/100	GENTLENESS	/100
LONG LIFE	/100	OBEDIENCE	/100

My highs and lows:

_____

_____

_____

_____

_____

_____

PROPHETS CROSSWORD

Look up answers in "Warning and Hope!" in *The Blockbuster Bible*. Complete the crossword with capital letters. Use a pencil in case you're wrong!

ACROSS

6 Jerusalem's proud king who ignores Jeremiah. (8)

7 The name for the people of God who Ezekiel speaks to. (5)

9 Daniel is thrown into a den of these. (5)

12 Elijah speaks against this king of Israel. (4)

13 This man leads his people in rebuilding Jerusalem's walls. (8)

14 This place is supposed to kill Daniels's friends. (5,7)

15 Daniel and his friends eat these instead of the king's food. (10)

16 Isaiah helps this king of Judah. (8)

18 Jeremiah warns this kingdom about destruction. (5)

19 Elijah shows who the real God is here. (5,6)

20 A man serious about teaching God's law after 70 years in Babylon. (4)

DOWN

1 The prophet who raises a widow's son. (6)

2 God's prophet in Babylon who acts out God's warnings. (7)

3 The false god who God's people often worship. (4)

4 This Assyrian king's massive army suddenly die. (11)

5 This king begs Daniel to explain a message. (10)

8 Nebuchadnezzar builds this for his kingdom to worship. (6,6)

10 The moaning prophet who sails away from Nineveh. (5)

11 This foreign kingdom destroys Judah. (7)

17 The Jewish queen of Xerxes. (6)

Line up these dates and events in the right order. How quickly can you do it?

Use p. 71 and 74–84, 90–91 of *The Blockbuster Bible* to help you.

Assyria invades Israel	**Isaiah warns and reassures Israel**
Jeremiah warns Judah and its kings	**Ezekiel speaks hope for the exiles**
The Northern Kingdom of Israel falls	**The Southern Kingdom of Judah falls**
The Exiles return from Babylon	**Babylon invades Judah**
Solomon dies: the kingdom divides in two	**722 BC**
586 BC	**538 BC**

1) Solomon dies: the kingdom divides in two; 2) Isaiah warns and reassures Israel; 3) Assyria invades Israel; 4) 722 BC; 5) The Northern Kingdom of Israel falls; 6) Jeremiah warns Judah and its kings; 7) Babylon invades Judah; 8) 586 BC; 9) The Southern Kingdom of Judah falls; 10) Ezekiel speaks hope for the exiles; 11) 538 BC; 12) The Exiles return from Babylon

CITYCHAT PAGE

Create a conversation happening in a city between several people. Draw character pictures, write their messages, and draw the photos they upload. The characters don't have to be friends!

CITY CHAT

◻ **PHOTOS**

☺ **FRIENDS**

🕐 **EVENTS**

@ LOCATION _____

SNAPSCROLL PAGE

Create a photo stream conversation happening in a city between several people.

Draw the photo uploads and write the character's comment on their picture.

📷 Snapscroll @location _____

1

Comment:

2

Comment:

3

Comment:

4

Comment:

5

Comment:

6

Comment:

7

Comment:

8

Comment:

9

Comment:

EMESSENGER PAGE

Craft an email between characters, or even many people. Use paragraphs:
1st paragraph – give the reason for writing; 2nd paragraph – describe the situation; 3rd paragraph – tell them what to do!

✉ eMessenger

From:

To:

Subject:

Picture:

LIVESTREAM PAGE

Report the latest event online. Begin at the bottom with what happened first, and then work up the page to what just happened. Add the times for events and add a picture that sums up the biggest moment. Say what you saw and what characters said.

▶ **LIVESTREAM**

Picture:

❚❚ ▶ ■   **LIVE @location** _____

Coverage:

_____ **ago**
_____
_____

_____ **ago**
_____
_____

_____ **ago**
_____
_____

_____ **ago**
_____
_____

_____ **ago**
_____
_____

_____ **ago**
_____
_____

MESSIANIC MATCHING PAIRS

Play matching pairs to compare the prophecy with its fulfilment. Cut out the boxes and turn them over on your desk. Don't read the prophecies until you're playing! Use p. 92–95 of *The Blockbuster Bible* to help you.

"A virgin will become pregnant! She will have a son and call him Immanuel – 'God is with us'."

"A child is born, called Wonderful Counsellor, Mighty God, Everlasting Father, Prince of Peace."

"Bethlehem! O small village! A ruler will come from you from the distant past."

"Rejoice, Jerusalem! Your king is coming! He rides lowly and victorious on a young donkey, a colt."

"I will be his father and he will be my son. I will make your family line and kingdom last forever."

"The Chosen One will die without a single possession."

"They will divide my clothes among them and cast lots for my clothing."

"Like sheep, we have all gone astray, we have all gone our own way; the Lord laid on him the sin of us all."

What is Isaiah talking about? Cut out the boxes and arrange them down the middle of your page. When your teacher says it is correct, you can stick them in. Read the boxes carefully! Use p. 95 of *The Blockbuster Bible* to help you.

FOR OUR REBELLION AND HIS SUFFERINGS BROUGHT US HAVE HEALED US.

BUT HE WAS PIERCED CRUSHED FOR OUR SINS! PEACE, AND HIS WOUNDS

AND THE LORD LAID ON HIM THE SIN OF US ALL.

OF US TURNED TO OUR OWN WAY,

WE ALL, LIKE SHEEP, HAVE GONE ASTRAY. ALL

HE CARRIED OUR SUFFERINGS! WE THOUGHT GOD PUNISHED HIM FOR HIS OWN SINS,

Now explain Isaiah's words. Who or what is he talking about?

Script keywords

Pierced

Sufferings

Like sheep

Laid on him

BIG CLAIMS

People have said big things about Jesus. Connect the quote with the speaker. Use an Internet search engine to help you. On the lines explain what this person thinks about Jesus. Why do they think Jesus is special?

> Either this man was, and is, the Son of God, or else a madman or something worse. You can shut him up for a fool, you can spit at him and kill him as a demon or you can fall at his feet and call him Lord and God.

C. S. Lewis – author of *The Lion, the Witch and the Wardrobe* (1950)

_____

_____

_____

_____

> He lived... as a greater artist than all other artists... That is to say... [he] made neither statues nor pictures nor books; he loudly proclaimed that he made... living men, immortals.

Napoleon Bonaparte – French conqueror in 1800s

_____

_____

_____

> I am the way and the truth and the life. There's no way to God except by me.

Albert Einstein – Jewish scientist in 1900s

_____

_____

_____

> I am a Jew, but I am enthralled by the luminous figure of the Nazarene.... No one can read the Gospels without feeling the actual presence of Jesus. His personality pulsates in every word. No myth is filled with such life.

Vincent van Gogh – Dutch painter in 1800s

_____

_____

_____

_____

> Jesus Christ is no mere man. Between Him and every person in the world there is no possible term of comparison. Alexander, Caesar, Charlemagne, and I have founded empires. But on what did we rest the creations of our genius? Upon force. Jesus Christ founded His Empire upon love; and at this hour millions... would die for him.

Jesus – carpenter, teacher, miracle maker, servant leader

_____

_____

_____

_____

_____

FAMILY TREE MAKING

Track back to Jesus' roots by making his family tree. Cut out and match up these names and pictures, then lay them out in time order (two columns). Challenge yourself: have a go and use p. 98 of *The Blockbuster Bible* to help you. Which names are most important? Write a description of each character.

Abraham

Jesus

David

Mary

Jacob

Solomon

Joseph

Rahab

Sarah

Boaz

Bathsheba

Adam

Isaac

Judah

Ruth

Jesse

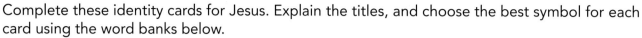

ID CARDS

Complete these identity cards for Jesus. Explain the titles, and choose the best symbol for each card using the word banks below.

SON OF ABRAHAM

"Son of Abraham" means… (p. 98)

"A son of" means … (p. 98)

MESSIAH

"Messiah" means… (p. 98)

Isaiah called the Messiah… (p. 100)

SON OF DAVID

"Son of David" means… (p. 98)

Micah said that in Bethlehem… (p. 101)

JESUS

"Jesus" means… (p. 99)

He was given this title by… (p. 99)

SON OF GOD

"Son of God" means… (p. 99)

At Jesus' baptism, God said… (p. 103)

IMMANUEL

"Immanuel" means… (p. 99)

Mary was made pregnant by… (p. 99)

Crown   *DNA*   *Stars*   *Two Hands*   *Rescue Ring*   *Oil on Head*

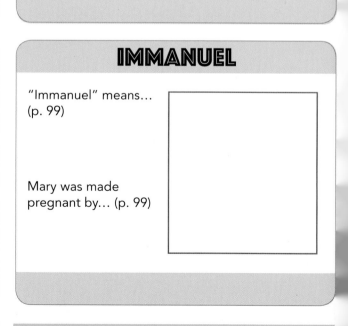

CAST AND CREW

Perform a scene and repeat it until everyone's happy with it. Fill in these cast slips with character names and their actions/speech.

The crew slips will help when acting the scene.

Character: _____
Actions or speech: _____
_____

Character: _____
Actions or speech: _____
_____

Character: _____
Actions or speech: _____
_____

Character: _____
Actions or speech: _____
_____

Character: _____
Actions or speech: _____
_____

Character: _____
Actions or speech: _____
_____

Character: _____
Actions or speech: _____
_____

Character: _____
Actions or speech: _____
_____

Character: _____
Actions or speech: _____
_____

Character: _____
Actions or speech: _____
_____

Character: _____
Actions or speech: _____
_____

Character: _____
Actions or speech: _____
_____

Character: _____
Actions or speech: _____
_____

Character: _____
Actions or speech: _____
_____

DIRECTOR
Tension, atmosphere, speed?

PRODUCER
Props, sound effects, costumes

SCRIPTWRITER
Lines, words, improvising speech?

ACTOR'S UNDERSTUDY
Swap in, change the acting style?

SCRIPTWRITER
Lines, words, improvising speech?

ACTOR'S UNDERSTUDY
Swap in, change the acting style?

GOSSIP COLUMN

Complete a magazine article on recent or exciting things a character has done; and on what others are saying about them. Use p. 104 of *The Blockbuster Bible* for the layout.

FURIOUS PHARISEES

You are a Pharisee and Jesus has just criticized you. Describe what he said and what it means. Write angrily and stubbornly! Use p. 109 of *The Blockbuster Bible* to help you.

List all the names and things Jesus called you.

How do you apparently stop people going to heaven?

What's apparently wrong with what you give to the poor? What do you forget?

Explain this: "You stretch out a fly, but shrink and swallow a camel!"

GUESS WHO

Create cards for characters and play "Guess Who". List character options in the boxes below. Then complete six picture cards showing their looks and a prop. Take turns to ask yes/no questions about your opponent's choice. If you guess their character correctly, or if they guess yours incorrectly, you win!

Perform Jesus' miracles with still poses for each scene. Circle the character you will play, and then write the expression you will use. Stay the same character throughout.

JESUS' MIRACLES

SCENE 1: Water into wine
Mary has told **Jesus** there is no wine, who tells the **servants** to fill water jars…

The **master of the feast** and **guests** love the wine! EXPRESSION: _____

SCENE 2: The paralysed man
Four people bring a **paralysed man** to **Jesus**, who forgives him and then heals him.

The **religious leaders** complain, and the **crowd** are amazed! EXPRESSION: _____

SCENE 3: Calming the storm
A storm has hit the **disciples**' boats. They are frightened of the storm, but terrified

of **Jesus**, who tells the storm to be quiet! EXPRESSION: _____

SCENE 4: Feeding the 5,000
Huge crowds have no food, so **Jesus** tells his **disciples** to feed them. He hands out

five loaves and two fish to feed everyone! EXPRESSION: _____

SCENE 5: Raising Lazarus
Martha and **Mary** have asked **Jesus** to heal dying **Lazarus**. Jesus comes late and

raises him from the dead! **Family** and **friends** watch on. EXPRESSION: _____

SCENE 6: The transfiguration
Peter, **James**, and **John** follow **Jesus** up a mountain, where his clothes turn bright white

and he meets **Moses** and **Elijah**. Peter wants to make tents! EXPRESSION: _____

SCENE 7: Healing Bartimaeus
Blind Bartimaeus calls **Jesus** the Son of David, but the **crowds** try to shut him up.

Jesus calls him over and heals him for his faith. EXPRESSION: _____

SCENE 8: Casting out a demon
Crowds bring a blind/mute **demon-possessed man** to **Jesus**, who heals him.

The **Pharisees** complain, but Jesus corrects them. EXPRESSION: _____

*agony shock compassion thoughtfulness hopelessness relief anger
desperation confusion blankness panic love hunger worry grief
delight calmness terror*

Sort these powers in a few ways. First cut them out, then order them by:

1) Most impressive 2) Most want to witness 3) Most helpful 4) Most surprising 5) Most important

Use p. 110–117 of *The Blockbuster Bible* to help you.

Draw one more…

REASON FOR RANKING (Most _____)

I have chosen this order because…

_____

_____

_____

_____

_____

_____

Report about Jesus' miracles around Galilee. Cover his 5 powers (over sin, sickness, nature, death, and demons). Use p. 110–117 of *The Blockbuster Bible* to help you.

 # THE GALILEE GAZETTE

Sum up the whole story with a headline:

All superpowers: *Jesus has God's powers!*

_____
_____
_____
_____
_____

One superpower:

_____
_____
_____
_____
_____

Another superpower:

_____
_____
_____
_____
_____

Things eyewitnesses say:

_____
_____
_____
_____
_____

Picture:

Picture caption:

Any other miracles:

_____
_____
_____
_____
_____

Other headlines:

_____
_____
_____
_____

Complete this certificate to tell how Lazarus came back to life. Report the story details and state what witnesses have told you. Write with alarm; you've never written one of these before! Use p. 114 of *The Blockbuster Bible* to help you.

LIFE CERTIFICATE

This certifies that _____

_____ is alive and that he/she has signed in my presence.

Other family: _____

How raised to life: _____

_____

_____

Witnesses present: _____

_____

_____

Additional notes: _____

_____

Signed: _____

Raised person signed: _____

CHARACTER ASSESSMENT

Read the parable of The Pharisee and the Tax Collector. Discuss what each character is like. Use the categories below. Use p. 121 of *The Blockbuster Bible* to help you.

THE TAX COLLECTOR

Body language?
(What is he doing? Where is he looking?)

Tone of voice?
(How does he speak? Volume? Speed? Feelings?)

Attitude to God and other people?
(How would he compare himself to God and other people?)

THE PHARISEE

Body language?
(What is he doing? Where is he looking?)

Tone of voice?
(How does he speak? Volume? Speed? Feelings?)

Attitude to God and other people?
(How would he compare himself to God and other people?)

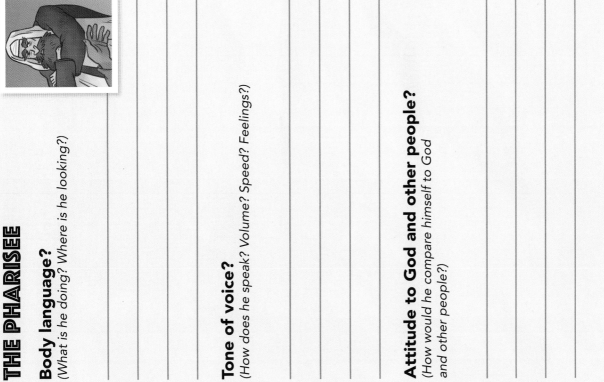

You are applying for the job of Good Shepherd. Answer these interview questions as yourself or as Jesus. Use p. 124 of *The Blockbuster Bible* to help you.

THE GOOD SHEPHERD

What do you think the job involves?

_____
_____
_____
_____

How is the Good Shepherd like a door?

_____
_____
_____
_____
_____
_____
_____

How will you be different from a thief?

_____
_____
_____
_____
_____
_____
_____

How far will you go in your job?

_____
_____
_____
_____
_____
_____

How will you gather one flock?

_____
_____
_____
_____
_____
_____

Perform the parable of The Farmers with still poses for each scene. Circle your character and plan your expression using the word bank. Use p. 125 of *The Blockbuster Bible* to help you.

THE PARABLE OF THE FARMERS

INTRO
The **owner** finishes the vineyard. He rents it to **tenants**, who must share the harvest.

EXPRESSION: _____

HARVEST TIME
A **servant** comes to collect fruit. The **tenants** plot to keep the harvest.

EXPRESSION: _____

BEATING
The **tenants** beat the **servant**. "Scram! It's all ours! And don't come back."

EXPRESSION: _____

EXPULSION
The **tenants** send away the **servant** empty-handed.

EXPRESSION: _____

SERVANT 2
A **second** servant arrives. The **tenants** hear him coming and get ready…

EXPRESSION: _____

SHAMING
The **tenants** shame the **second servant**. "Scram! No more of you! You'll learn."

EXPRESSION: _____

SERVANT 3
A **third servant** arrives. The **tenants** hear him coming and get ready…

EXPRESSION: _____

KILLING
The **tenants** kill the **third servant**.

EXPRESSION: _____

OWNER AND SON
The **owner** sends his **son**. "I can send one more. My Son. They will respect him."

EXPRESSION: _____

SON
The **son** arrives. The **tenants** kill him. "Look! The heir! Let's kill him and the vineyard will be ours!"

EXPRESSION: _____

OWNER
The **owner** comes to kill the **tenants**.

EXPRESSION: _____

*shock compassion giving hopeless relief anger desperation confusion
blank scared panic love vengeful worry grief calm terror*

Write your own Good Samaritan parable. Follow the same story structure to shock your audience with a modern retelling. Use p. 120 of *The Blockbuster Bible* to help you.

A MODERN GOOD SAMARITAN

Setting: Where and when are we?

_____

_____

_____

_____

1. Characters and problem
Who begins the story?
What's their situation?

_____

_____

_____

_____

_____

2. Surprising rejection
Who doesn't help?
Why?

_____

_____

_____

_____

_____

3. Surprising helper
Who does help?
Introduce them with "But…"

_____

_____

_____

_____

_____

4. Surprising generosity
How are they good?
Give lots of ways.

_____

_____

_____

_____

_____

Line up these events in the week leading up to when Jesus dies on the cross.
Arrange them across your page in rows. Use p. 126–135 of *The Blockbuster Bible* to help you.

The risen Jesus meets Mary in the garden	Rulers and soldiers mock Jesus as saviour	Jesus prays in the Garden of Gethsemane	A Roman centurion calls Jesus the Son of God
The Temple curtain tears in two	Pontius Pilate sends Jesus to die and washes his hands	Judas betrays Jesus to the rulers	Jesus gives the bread and wine
Planning death and resurrection	Jesus says, "It is finished."	Jesus rides into Jerusalem on a donkey	Peter denies knowing Jesus
Judas throws the silver back and hangs himself	Joseph and Nicodemus bury Jesus	The high priest condemns Jesus to death	Jesus washes the disciples' feet
A dying thief calls Jesus the king	Soldiers take Jesus to "The Skull"	Darkness fills the land for 3 hours	Jesus dies on the cross at 3 p.m.

Complete these conversations that happened when Jesus rode into Jerusalem. Use normal language, and show how the disciples misunderstand Jesus' plans, how the crowds understand Jesus' plans, and how the Pharisees are angry. Use p. 128 of *The Blockbuster Bible* to help you.

Jesus: You two! Find a young donkey in the village. No one has ridden it. Bring it here!

Disciples: Here it is, Jesus! Why did you want a donkey? You need a great horse!

Disciples: _____

Jesus: _____

Crowds: _____

Crowds: _____

Crowds: They are a sign of victory. And the street is dusty! It's not fit for a king! Come on, help out!

Crowds: Who? Of course, he's the prophet Jesus, from Nazareth in Galilee! Join in!

Pharisees: Why are these people singing like this?! Who do you think you are?!

Pharisees: Tell these people to be quiet! You've lost control!

Jesus: _____

Jesus: _____

STAGE DIRECTIONS

Complete the scene of Jesus' crucifixion. Add speech bubbles and draw anything else that happens. Don't forget to label the characters and extra drawings. Use p. 132–133 of *The Blockbuster Bible* to help you.

Look up answers in "Act 6: The Promised King" in *The Blockbuster Bible*. Complete the crossword with capital letters. Use a pencil in case you're wrong!

ACROSS

1 Jesus makes this from water. (4)

4 A tax collector who drops everything to follow Jesus. (4)

5 The close friend who denies knowing Jesus at his trials. (5)

6 This foreign lady finds Jesus to be the messiah. (9)

13 Jesus feeds this to 5,000 men, plus women and children. (5,3,4)

14 The man whom Jesus raises from the dead. (7)

15 The blind man who sees who Jesus is. (10)

16 Jesus shouts at this, "Quiet! Be still!" (5)

17 Jesus rides this into Jerusalem. (6)

18 Another name for disciples. (9)

DOWN

1 The first people to find Jesus' empty tomb. (5)

2 Jesus chooses these people as his first disciples. (9)

3 Jesus is a Son of… (7)

5 Jesus teaches these to his followers. (8)

7 A title for Jesus at his birth meaning "God is with us". (8)

8 A title from Jesus' family tree meaning Chosen One. (6)

9 Jesus shows this to Peter, James, and John on a mountain. (5)

10 The man who believes when he sees Jesus die. (9)

11 Jesus forgives this man, who wants to be healed. (9)

12 These people oppose Jesus and his teaching (9)

HOLY WEEK SNAKES AND LADDERS

Follow Jesus through the week of his death and resurrection.
Watch out for those chief priests and faithless disciples!

At a snake or ladder, answer your classmates' question to avoid sliding down, or to climb up!

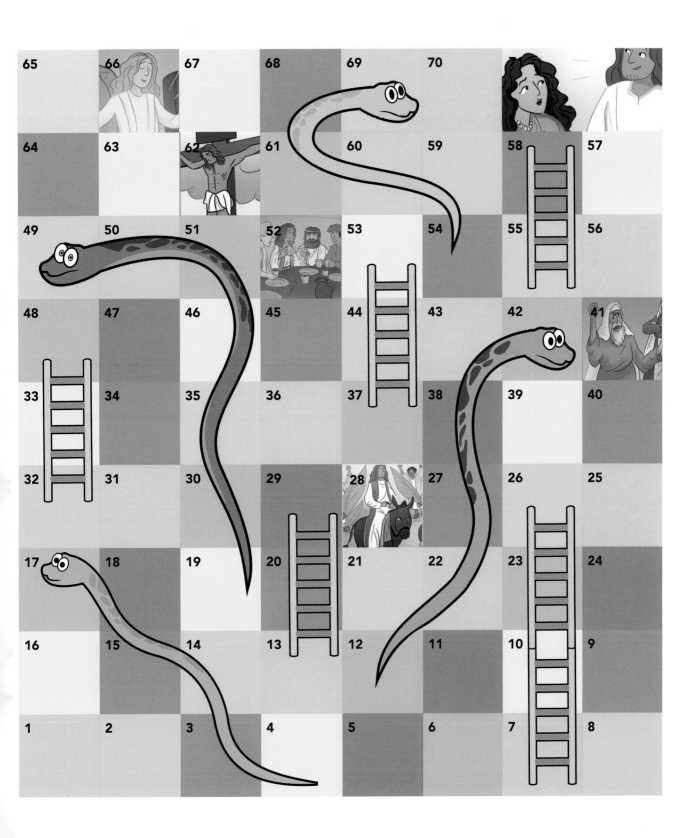

HEADLINE WRITING

Craft 2 short and catchy headlines for each of these events. Use names and places, and use short English (no "a" or "the")! Carefully read the story details, using p. 140–141 of *The Blockbuster Bible* to help you.

BREAKING NEWS!

_____

JESUS PROMISES HOLY SPIRIT IN
JERUSALEM MISSION

I promise you: I will stay with you always, to the very end of the world.

BREAKING NEWS!

MIRACLE MASTER JESUS MAKES
MESSENGERS FOR ALL NATIONS!

_____

I command you: go and make disciples in all nations!

BREAKING NEWS!

_____

At Pentecost a loud sound like a mighty rushing wind filled the house and tongues of fire rested on the disciples' heads.

BREAKING NEWS!

_____

Listen! Jesus will return in the same way he left. Stay in Jerusalem until the Holy Spirit comes!

BREAKING NEWS!

_____

The Holy Spirit filled the disciples and they spoke in many different languages. Then they explained the good news.

NEWS TEAM

Prepare a news report so it's ready to perform.
Perform it using the order numbered on the 3 cards.

NEWSREADER

1. Opening description
(What has happened? Event names?)

2. Handover to reporter
(What will the reporter explain?)

9. Closing remarks
(What have we learned?)

REPORTER

3. Finer details
(Names? Places? Stories?)

4. Interview questions
(Events? What was said? Understanding why?)

8. Hand-back to newsreader
(What has surprised you?)

PASSER-BY

5. Eyewitness details
(What was said? What surprised you?)

6. Opinions
(Why do you think it happened?)

7. Impact
(How has the event affected you?)

Design a storyboard on how Paul met Jesus on the road to Damascus. Write titles for each shot, draw the shots, and write the speech below. Add any extra arrows and descriptions you want, like in box 1. Use a pen for writing and colour it in last. Use p. 146 of *The Blockbuster Bible* to help you.

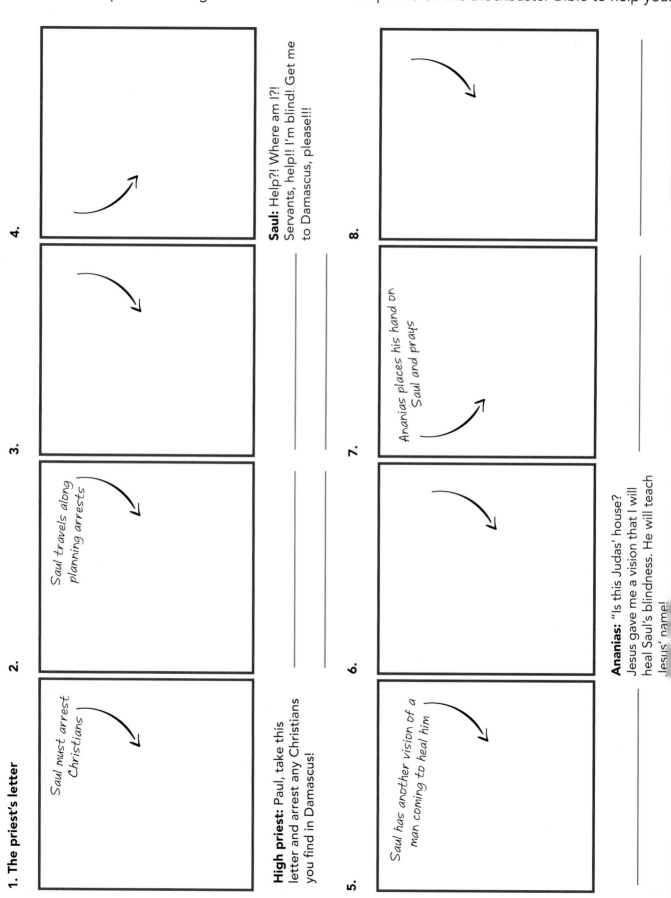

1. The priest's letter

Saul must arrest Christians

High priest: Paul, take this letter and arrest any Christians you find in Damascus!

2.

Saul travels along planning arrests

3.

Saul: Help?! Where am I?! Servants, help!! I'm blind! Get me to Damascus, please!!!

4.

5.

Saul has another vision of a man coming to heal him

6.

Ananias: "Is this Judas' house? Jesus gave me a vision that I will heal Saul's blindness. He will teach Jesus' name!

7.

Ananias places his hand on Saul and prays

8.

BREAKING NEWS SCREEN

Design news screens for two stories. Be ready to hold up the screen and narrate the story for a news report. How long can you speak for?

LIVE @location _____

Scene picture

News channel name	
Super-catchy headline	
Subheading	
Scrolling text: 3–4 word phrases, max. 4 words	
Quotes	

LIVE @location _____

Scene picture

News channel name	
Super-catchy headline	
Subheading	
Scrolling text: 3–4 word phrases, max. 4 words	
Quotes	

Read John's interview about the new creation. Imagine you are John and you want to tell a friend what you saw. Write a postcard telling them everything! Use p. 152 of *The Blockbuster Bible* to help you.

Deliver to:
All people,
All nations,
All of time,
Planet Earth.

Dear...
I had a revelation! I saw...

On the throne...

It's like the Passover...

God keeps his promises! He...

Yours,

HOME SWEET HOME PICTURE

Read John's interview about the new creation. Draw all the things he saw and label everything. Use p. 152–154 of *The Blockbuster Bible* to help you.

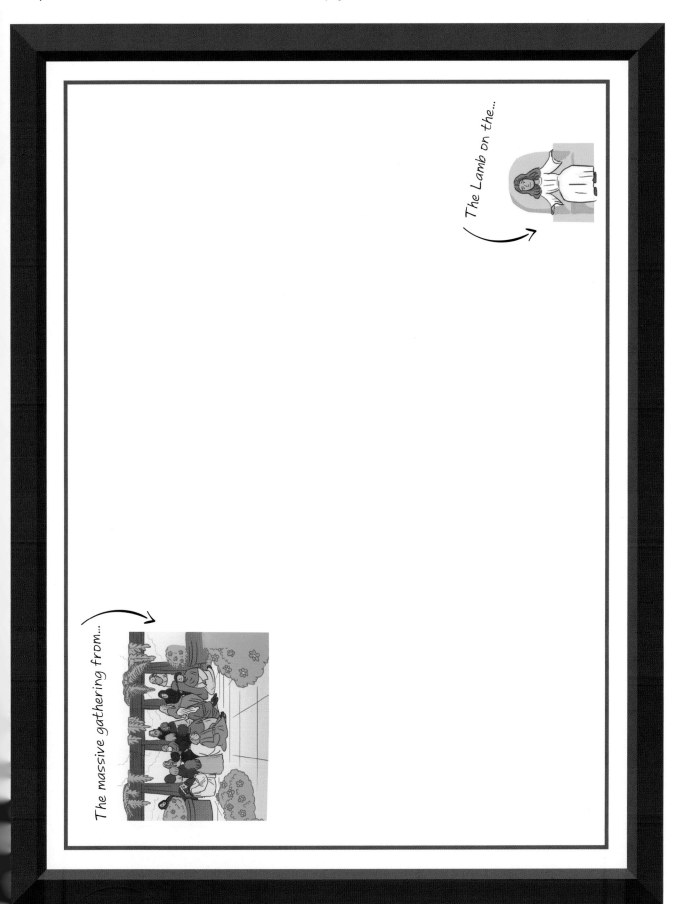

The Lamb on the...

The massive gathering from...

SORTING SENTENCES 2

Cut out and organize 5 sentences describing God's new Eden. Each one has 3 boxes. When you are finished stick them into your book and draw a symbol for each of the descriptions, trying to sum up the whole meaning of each description. Use p. 154 of *The Blockbuster Bible* to help you.

God and the Lamb Jesus on the	God walked in the Garden with	crops of fruit, one per month.
Its leaves heal the nations.	clear as crystal, running	The massive
gathering reign as kings	throne in the city. He	man and woman, and they looked after it.
no longer curses anything.	The river of the water of life,	for ever and ever.
Flashback... to Eden. There was a river and a tree of life.	The tree of life, with twelve	from God's throne through the middle of the city.

TOURIST BROCHURE

FLEXI-TASK

Complete a leaflet to advertize the place where God's people live in the new creation.
Invite the reader to this place with some fun taglines and exciting descriptions.

THINGS TO DO

Tagline

PEOPLE TO MEET

Tagline

SIGHTS

Tagline

Recap the story of Living with God. Cut out the pictures and the captions, and then match them up and arrange them in time order. Then stick them down!

God and the Lamb Jesus rule from the throne	God leads Israel to the Promised Land	God lives with Adam and Eve	Immanuel ("God is with us") is born
God banishes Adam and Eve	God lives in the tabernacle; sacrifices pay for sins	God promises to bless Abraham's people	Jesus performs God's powers
God calls Jesus his Son at his baptism	God lives in the Temple	God sends Cain further away	Shepherds and wise men bow to Jesus
God exiles his people to Babylon	God lives with a massive gathering in the new Jerusalem	God the Father rejects Jesus at the cross	The Holy Spirit comes to live inside God's people

Recap the story of *God's Promises*. Draw lines to match God's promise with its fulfilment. Then explain how God fulfils each promise. One has been done for you.

God's promise	Fulfilment	How God fulfils his Promise
One of Eve's descendants will crush the snake's head, but it will strike his heel to kill him		**Massive gathering**
Abraham, I will give this land to you and to your children after you: the land of Canaan.		**Jesus returns**
Abraham, I will make you into a great nation. I will multiply you.		**Map of Israel** *The nation of Israel conquers Canaan and divides the land between the tribes*
Abraham, I will bless all the nations on earth through one of your descendants.		**Lamb Jesus on throne**
David, I will make your family line and kingdom last forever.		**The Cross**
I promise, I am coming soon!		**Nation Israel**

Recap the story of *God's Rescue*. Plot a line showing the friendship between God and his people across the Bible story. Add small drawings along the way.

Chart 1

Row labels:
- **Perfectly loving God**
- **Walking with God for now**
- **Turning away from God**
- **Rejecting God**

Columns (left to right):
- Adam and Eve rule creation under God.
- Adam and Eve rebel against God.
- God sends Cain further away.
- Abraham obeys God's instructions.
- Israel suffers as slaves in Egypt.
- Israel lives with God at the tabernacle.
- Israel complains; God sends snakes.
- Moses sets up the bronze snake.
- 12 spies explore the Promised Land.
- Israel prefers Egypt; wander for 40 years.
- Joshua leads Israel into Canaan.
- Israel worships any god; God brings enemies.

Chart 2

Continue your line

Row labels:
- **Perfectly loving God**
- **Walking with God for now**
- **Turning away from God**
- **Rejecting God**

Columns (left to right):
- Judges lead Israel to defeat enemies.
- King Saul leads for himself, not for God.
- King David leads Israel to love God.
- Israel worships at Solomon's Temple.
- Solomon worships foreign gods.
- Kings mostly disobey; prophets warn.
- God exiles Judah to Babylon.
- Shepherds and wise men worship Jesus.
- Crowds follow; Pharisees oppose Jesus.
- Jesus is crucified but he rises from the dead.
- Risen Jesus sends disciples to all nations.
- A massive gathering worships God.

Recap The Big Story of the Bible using these 24 images. Arrange them in the correct order, then, on the back, see if you can write the names of characters from their scenes. Use p. 4–5 of *The Blockbuster Bible* if you really need to!

 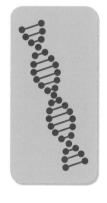   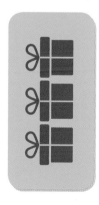 

CROSSWORD ANSWERS PAGE

Covenants Crossword

ACROSS
4 REST
5 MOSAIC
7 SPECIAL
9 SNAKE
10 DAVIDIC
11 LAND
14 MOUNT SINAI
15 PROMISES
16 NATION
18 ABRAHAMIC
19 BLESSING

DOWN
1 FATHER
2 PEOPLE
3 MOSES
6 REMINDER
7 SABBATH
8 WEDDING
12 COVENANTS
13 RAINBOW
17 NOAHIC

Judges and Kings Crossword

ACROSS
6 JAEL
7 GIDEON
8 DELILAH
10 QUEEN OF SHEBA
12 SAMUEL
13 WEAK
15 EGLON
16 HAIR
17 SAMSON

DOWN
1 SAUL
2 WISDOM
3 EHUD
4 BATHSHEBA
5 JAWBONE
6 JONATHAN
7 GOLIATH
8 DEBORAH
9 TEMPLE
11 FOREIGN
14 JESSE

Prophets Crossword

ACROSS
6 ZEDEKIAH
7 EXILES
9 LIONS
12 AHAB
13 NEHEMIAH
14 FIERY FURNACE
15 VEGETABLES
16 HEZEKIAH
18 JUDAH
19 MOUNT CARMEL
20 EZRA

DOWN
1 ELIJAH
2 EZEKIEL
3 BAAL
4 SENNACHERIB
5 BELSHAZZAR
8 GOLDEN STATUE
10 JONAH
11 BABYLON
17 ESTHER

The Promised King Crossword

ACROSS
1 WINE
4 LEVI
5 PETER
6 SAMARITAN
13 BREAD AND FISH
14 LAZARUS
15 BARTIMAEUS
16 STORM
17 DONKEY
18 FOLLOWERS

DOWN
1 WOMEN
2 FISHERMEN
3 ABRAHAM
5 PARABLES
7 IMMANUEL
8 CHRIST
9 GLORY
10 CENTURION
11 PARALYSED
12 PHARISEES